SIGNIFICANT DECISIONS
OF THE SUPREME COURT
1972-73 Term

Bruce E. Fein

AMERICAN ENTERPRISE INSTITUTE
For Public Policy Research
1150 17th Street, N.W., Washington, D.C. 20036

Bruce E. Fein, a graduate of Harvard Law School and a former clerk to a U.S. district judge, is a member of the California Bar and the American Bar Association.

Special Analysis No. 29, July 1974
Price $3.00 per copy

Library of Congress Catalog Card Number L.C. 74-79273
ISBN O-8447-1073-3

CONTENTS

OVERVIEW

The Supreme Court's record for the 1972-73 term, the first full term during which four Nixon appointees were on the bench, supports the impression of many observers that the "Burger Court" has embarked on a more conservative course than that followed by the "Warren Court." Justice Byron White, a Kennedy appointee, provided the crucial swing vote in many of the Court's controversial decisions. Indeed, in the final weeks of the Court's term, 18 decisions turned on 5-4 votes and White sided with the conservative majority in all but two of the cases. Chief Justice Warren E. Burger, and his colleagues Harry A. Blackmun, Lewis F. Powell, Jr., and William H. Rehnquist, all Nixon appointees, voted together on 70 percent of the cases heard and decided during the term, virtually always in the majority. Justices William O. Douglas, William J. Brennan, Jr., and Thurgood Marshall also voted together 70 percent of the time, often in dissent. Justice White voted with the four Nixon appointees 94 percent of the time that they voted together, while the corresponding figure for Justice Potter Stewart, an Eisenhower appointee, was 74 percent.

Justice Douglas cast the most dissenting votes—70. Justices Brennan and Marshall were his nearest rivals with 49 and 46 dissenting votes, respectively. Justices Powell and Blackmun most frequently joined majority opinions and dissented only 11 times each. Justices Stewart and Rehnquist dissented 34 and 33 times, respectively. The Chief Justice and Justice White dissented 19 times.

While a generally conservative trend was indicated, the landmark decisions of the 1972-73 term did not display any notable consistency. On the controversial abortion question, on which state legislatures had been moving with relative speed toward some liberalization, the Court stepped in to strike down anti-abortion laws in 46 states and held that a woman has a virtually unlimited right to have an abortion during the first six months of pregnancy. On the other hand, the Court refused to strike down a state scheme of financing public education on the ground, among others, that it was unwilling to assume a wisdom superior to that of legislators, scholars, and educational authorities in 49 states.

Observing the lack of evidence showing that the nineteenth century censorship of public distribution and display of materials relating to sex limited or affected in any way the expression of serious literary, artistic, political or scientific ideas,

1

Chief Justice Burger, writing for a 5-4 majority, ushered in an era of tighter controls on obscenity in a series of cases. A 1966 Court ruling had held that materials could not be judged obscene if they had some "redeeming social value." The Chief Justice rewrote the constitutional definition of obscenity to cover any materials which appeal to a prurient interest in sex, which portray specifically defined sexual conduct in a patently offensive way and which, taken as a whole, do not have serious literary, artistic, political or scientific value. Under the Burger definition of obscenity, local standards determine the meaning of what is "prurient" or "patently offensive." Thus materials may be deemed constitutionally obscene in some places and not in others.

In a decision having no precedential effect, the Court, on the basis of a finding that the city of Richmond, Virginia, had unconstitutionally segregated schools, divided 4-4 over the issue of whether a federal district judge had the power to order two adjacent white suburban communities to participate in a desegregation plan designed to integrate Richmond schools. The tie vote had the effect of affirming a court of appeals ruling that had thrown out the proposed metropolitan school merger. That same basic issue will arise next term when a metropolitan desegregation plan centered on Detroit comes up for review. Justice Powell, who disqualified himself in the Richmond case because he had been a member of the state and city school boards, may cast the deciding vote in the Detroit case. In a major case involving the desegregation of Denver schools this term, Powell emphasized a desire to treat northern and southern school districts equally but also appears to have indicated a preference for local control over schools. Thus, how Powell will vote in the Detroit case is still a question mark.

The justices were also deadlocked 4-4 in a controversial case involving the interpretation of federal pollution laws. This tie vote left standing a lower court decision that federal law does not allow states to permit air quality deterioration in relatively clean areas, even though the deterioration would not result in a violation of federal pollution standards set for already polluted areas.

The Court ended any hope of providing substantial state aid to parochial schools in striking down, by 6-3 majorities, tax credit and tuition reimbursement schemes aiding parents who send their children to nonpublic schools. Federal income tax credits for parents sending children to nonpublic schools would thus seem unconstitutional under the latest Court rulings.

In the field of reapportionment, the Court displayed some inconsistency in relaxing the constitutional one-man, one-vote standards as applied to states, while tightening those standards as applied to federal congressional elections.

Federal Rules of Evidence. On November 20, 1972, the Supreme Court sent to Congress proposed Federal Rules of Evidence to be generally applicable to federal courts beginning July 1, 1973. Justice Douglas dissented on the grounds that the Supreme Court was both unauthorized and unqualified to propose such rules. Some of the proposed rules were highly controversial, especially those dealing with the withholding of information concerning state secrets and other official information. For this reason and others, Congress passed a statute forbidding any of the proposed rules from taking effect unless Congress affirmatively approves them. To date Congress has not taken final action on any of the proposed rules.

Caseload. Because of the Court's increasing caseload, the Chief Justice in the fall of 1971 appointed a group of legal experts, headed by Professor Paul A. Freund of Harvard Law School, to study the caseload of the Supreme Court and to make such recommendations as its findings warranted. In December 1972, the group reported its findings and made the following recommendations:

1. The establishment by statute of a National Court of Appeals, with a membership of seven judges drawn on a rotating basis from the federal courts of appeals and serving staggered three-year terms. This Court would have the twofold function of (1) screening all petitions for certiorari and appeals that would at present be filed in the Supreme Court, referring the most review-worthy (perhaps 400 or 450 per Term) to the Supreme Court (except as provided in clause (2)), and denying the rest; and (2) retaining for decision on the merits cases of genuine conflict between circuits (except those of special moment, which would be certified to the Supreme Court). The Supreme Court would determine which of the cases thus referred to it should be granted review and decided on the merits in the Supreme Court. The residue would be denied, or in some instances remanded for decision by the National Court of Appeals.

2. The elimination by statute of three-judge district courts and direct review of their decisions in the Supreme Court; the elimination also of direct appeals in ICC and antitrust cases; and the substitution of certiorari for appeal in all cases where appeal is now the prescribed procedure for review in the Supreme Court. This recommendation is not dependent on the adoption of the preceding recommendation. If a National Court of Appeals is established, these recommended changes in appellate procedure would become applicable to it.

3. The establishment by statute of a non-judicial body whose members would investigate and report on complaints of prisoners, both collateral attacks on convictions and complaints of mistreatment in prison. Recourse to this procedure would be available to prisoners before filing a petition in a federal court, and to the federal judges with whom petitions were filed.

4. Increased staff support for the Supreme Court in the Clerk's office and the Library, and improved secretarial facilities for the Justices and their law clerks.[1]

---

[1] *Report of the Study Group on the Caseload of the Supreme Court* (Washington, D.C.: Federal Judicial Center, 1972), pp. 47-48.

1972-73 Statistics. The caseload of the Supreme Court set a new record again this term with a total of 4,640 cases on the docket. The Court also produced a record 159 decisions with full opinions, and disposed of a record 3,748 cases, leaving 892 cases on the docket for the next term.

A brief description of the Court's significant decisions in each area precedes a case-by-case summary.

SUMMARIES OF SIGNIFICANT DECISIONS

Due Process

The most controversial decisions of this term struck down almost all restrictions on abortion during the first three months of pregnancy, permitted restrictions during the middle three months only if necessary to preserve the mother's life or health, and authorized restrictions during the last three months to protect the fetus as well as the mother. The Court's 7-2 decisions were based upon a woman's fundamental right of privacy which the Court derived from the general spirit of the Constitution and from various clauses within it. These decisions stimulate speculation as to whether a state might constitutionally proscribe an abortion if sought during the first six months of pregnancy for the purpose of destroying a fetus's right of inheritance under an existing will and to enhance the mother's corresponding rights under that will. An even more perplexing question is whether the Court's abortion decisions permit states to prohibit payments by doctors to women for their consent to have an abortion in return for the doctor's experimental use of the fetus.

In past years the Court had moved away from striking down legislation on the ground that it was so arbitrary as to violate due process. Several justices thought that to do so was tantamount to making the Supreme Court a super-legislature. This term, however, the Court struck down on due process grounds an attempt by Congress to prohibit "hippies" and college students from wealthy families from participating in the food stamp program and an attempt by the state of Connecticut to continue to charge nonresident tuition rates to nonresident applicants to the state higher education system during all four years of college even if they become Connecticut residents during that time. In holding that certain armed forces benefit statutes unconstitutionally discriminated against women, four justices of the Court stated that sex-based discrimination could be upheld only if necessary to support a substantial or compelling governmental interest.

Roe v. Wade, 410 U.S. 113 (1973)

Facts: An unmarried pregnant woman, a licensed physician under prosecution in state court for violating the Texas abortion statutes, and a married couple challenged the constitutionality of Texas statutes making it a crime to "procure an abortion" except "for the purpose of saving the life of the mother," on the ground that the statutes violated a woman's right of privacy as protected by the First, Fourth, Fifth, Ninth and Fourteenth Amendments. Although holding the challenged statutes unconstitutional, a lower federal court concluded that the unmarried pregnant woman and the physician, but not the married couple, had standing to bring the suit.

Questions: Do the Texas abortion statutes violate a woman's constitutional right of privacy? Did the lower federal court properly hold that the unmarried pregnant woman and the licensed physician had standing, but that the married couple did not have standing to challenge the constitutionality of the Texas abortion statutes?

Decision: Only the unmarried pregnant woman and the licensed physician had standing to challenge the abortion statutes, but the lower federal court should have abstained from deciding the physician's claims. The Texas abortion statutes unconstitutionally violate a woman's right of privacy. Opinion by Justice Blackmun. Vote: 7-2.

Reasons: On the question of standing, the Court ruled that under Article III of the Constitution, the federal courts have jurisdiction to hear suits only when the litigants have a "personal stake in the outcome of the controversy . . . that insures that the dispute sought to be adjudicated will be presented in an adversary context and in a form historically viewed as capable of judicial resolution." Under this test, the unmarried pregnant woman clearly had a sufficient personal stake in the outcome of the controversy to give the lower federal court Article III jurisdiction to hear the suit. While noting that the woman was not pregnant at the time the Supreme Court heard the case and that the usual rule in federal suits is that an actual controversy must exist at all stages of litigation, the Court concluded that since the 266-day human gestation period would virtually always terminate before appellate review was complete in any given case, it was proper to hear the suit because otherwise issues involving pregnancy would be "capable of repetition, yet evad[e] review."

Regarding the standing of the licensed physician, the Court held that in the absence of harassment or bad faith in the pending state prosecution of him for allegedly violating the challenged abortion statutes, standards of comity between state and federal courts mandated that the lower federal court abstain from deciding his suit until the state courts heard his challenge to the constitutionality of the abortion statutes.

The married couple claimed standing on the theory that sometime in the future the wife might become pregnant because of the failure of contraceptive devices and that the knowledge that she might not get a legal abortion adversely affected their enjoyment of sexual relations. The Court held the married couple lacked standing to bring the suit because any alleged injury to them caused by the challenged abortion statute was too speculative, resting upon "possible future contraceptive failure, possible future pregnancy, possible future unpreparedness for parenthood, and possible future impairment of health."

Concerning the right to privacy, the Court held that only a "compelling" state interest could constitutionally justify impinging on this right, stating that the constitutional right of a woman to terminate her pregnancy without state interference was "fundamental" and protected by concepts of liberty and privacy embodied in the Due Process Clause of the Fourteenth Amendment. After tracing their origins and history, the Court concluded that criminal abortion laws were passed primarily to protect the safety of pregnant women when abortions were medically hazardous. Since medical advances have made abortion during the first trimester of pregnancy relatively safe and a fetus is not viable outside the mother during that period, the Court ruled that during the first three months of pregnancy a woman has a constitutional right to seek and get an abortion from a willing physician of her choice. In reaching this conclusion, the Court noted the following harms befalling a woman bearing an unwanted child:

> Maternity, or additional offspring, may force upon the woman a distressful life and future. Psychological harm may be imminent. Mental and physical health may be taxed by child care. There is also the distress, for all concerned, associated with the unwanted child, and there is the problem of bringing a child into a family already unable, psychologically and otherwise, to care for it. In other cases, as in this one, the additional difficulties and continuing stigma of unwed motherhood may be involved.

During the second trimester of pregnancy, when the medical danger of abortion is greater, the Court held that a state may constitutionally "regulate the abortion procedure to the extent that the regulation reasonably relates to the preservation and protection of maternal health":

> Examples of permissible state regulation in this area are requirements as to the qualifications of the person who is to perform the abortion; as to the licensure of that person; as to the facility in which the procedure is to be performed. . . .

Regarding the period that approximates the last trimester of pregnancy, the Court concluded that the state had a "compelling" interest in protecting the life of the fetus because during this time it "has the capability of meaningful life outside the mother's womb." Thus, the state may "proscribe abortion during that period except when it is necessary to preserve the life or health of the mother."

Because the challenged Texas abortion statutes did not meet constitutionally mandated standards based upon a tripartite division of pregnancy, the Court struck it down. However, the Court specifically left open the question of what a father's constitutional rights are in seeking to prevent an abortion.

Doe v. Bolton, 410 U.S. 179 (1973)

Facts: Georgia law proscribed an abortion except as performed by a duly licensed Georgia physician when necessary "in his best clinical judgment" because (1) continued pregnancy would endanger a pregnant woman's life or injure her health, (2) the fetus would likely be born with serious defects, or (3) the pregnancy resulted from rape. Additionally, the Georgia statutes permitted abortions for Georgia residents only and required (1) that the abortion be performed in a hospital accredited by the Joint Commission on Accreditation of Hospitals (2) that the abortion be approved by the hospital staff abortion committee, and (3) that the performing physician's decision to abort be confirmed by independent examination of the patient by two licensed physicians. A pregnant woman, licensed physicians, nurses, clergymen, social workers, and two nonprofit Georgia corporations supporting abortion reform challenged the constitutionality of the Georgia abortion statutes on the ground that they violated a woman's right of privacy. In striking down portions of the challenged abortion statute, a lower federal court held that only the pregnant woman could properly maintain the suit because the other plaintiffs did not allege a "justiciable controversy."

Questions: Did the physicians, nurses, social workers, clergymen, and non-profit corporations have standing to challenge the Georgia abortion law? Is the Georgia abortion statute unconstitutional?

Decision: The physicians and the pregnant woman had standing and thus it is unnecessary to decide whether the other plaintiffs had standing. The Georgia abortion statute is unconstitutional. Vote: 7-2.

Reasons: Regarding the standing issue, the Court held that because "[t]he physician is the one against whom these criminal statutes directly operate in the event he procures an abortion that does not meet the statutory exceptions and conditions . . . [the physicians] assert a sufficiently direct threat of personal detriment" to present a justiciable controversy and give them standing to challenge the constitutionality of the abortion statute. The Court further noted that

> [t]he parallel claims of the nurse, clergy, social worker, and corporation-appellants are another step removed and as to them, the Georgia statutes operate less directly. Not being licensed physicians, the nurses and the others are in no position to render medical advice. They would be reached by the abortion statutes only in their capacity as accessories or as counselor-conspirators. We conclude that we need not pass upon the status of these additional appellants in this suit, for the issues are sufficiently and adequately presented by [the physicians and pregnant woman in the suit].

Concerning the right-to-privacy contentions, the Court struck down portions of the abortion statute which, contrary to the Court's ruling in *Roe* v. *Wade,* 410 U.S. 113 (1973), restricted the right of a woman to have an abortion within the first trimester of pregnancy and which imposed restrictions on abortion during the second trimester unrelated to preserving the mother's physical or mental health. The statutory requirements invalidated were:

> (1) that the abortion be performed in a hospital accredited by the Joint Commission on Accreditation of Hospitals; (2) that the procedure be approved by the hospital staff abortion committee; and (3) that the

8

performing physician's judgment be confirmed by the independent examinations of the patient by two other licensed physicians.

The Court further held that Georgia's residency restriction deprived nonresidents of the same medical care to which Georgia residents were entitled, and thus violated Article IV, Section 2 of the Constitution providing that "[t]he Citizens of each State shall be entitled to all Privileges and Immunities of Citizens in the several States."

The Court rejected the contention, however, that provisions of the challenged Georgia statute were unconstitutionally vague in prohibiting abortions during the last trimester of pregnancy except when a physician "based upon his best clinical judgment [deems] that an abortion is necessary." The Court based this decision on *United States* v. *Vuitch,* 402 U.S. 62 (1971), in which it held that a District of Columbia statute forbidding abortions unless necessary to preserve the mother's physical or mental health was not unconstitutionally vague because physicians routinely made such judgments concerning a patient's health when performing other operations. In the instant case, the Court reasoned that because the challenged statute had been properly interpreted to permit a physician to consider all factors relevant to the woman's well-being in determining whether an abortion was "necessary"—physical, emotional, psychological, familial, and the woman's age—and because physicians frequently made these types of medical judgments in connection with other operations, the statute was not unconstitutionally vague.

Vlandis v. Kline, 412 U.S. 441 (1973)

Facts: A Connecticut statute required nonresidents enrolled in the state university system to pay higher tuition and fees than it required of resident students. Moreover, the statute created an irrebuttable presumption that unmarried persons who for any part of the one-year period immediately prior to their application for admission maintained a legal address outside the state of Connecticut would be considered nonresidents during their entire period of attendance in the state university system. Under the statute, a married person was conclusively deemed a nonresident during his (or her) entire attendance at any part of the state university system if his legal address was outside Connecticut at the time of his application for admission. The Connecticut statute was challenged as unconstitutional on the ground that the conclusive presumption of nonresidency against those students who acquired actual domicile within Connecticut during their attendance in part of the state university system was so arbitrary as to violate due process.

Question: Is the challenged Connecticut statute creating an irrebuttable presumption that an out-of-state applicant remains a nonresident for as long as he is a student in the state university system so arbitrary and unreasonable as to violate the Due Process Clause of the Fourteenth Amendment?

Decision: Yes. Opinion by Justice Stewart. Vote: 6-3.

Reasons: "Statutes creating permanent irrebuttable presumptions have long been disfavored under the Due Process Clause of the Fifth and Fourteenth Amend-

9

ments." In this case the state proffered three reasons to justify its challenged permanent, irrebuttable presumption of nonresidency: (1) to ensure that only bona fide Connecticut residents receive state subsidized education, (2) to ensure that only long-time Connecticut taxpayers or their children receive a state subsidized education, and (3) to provide administrative certainty in determining which persons are bona fide state residents. The first reason is invalid because the challenged statute prevents bona fide Connecticut residents from receiving a state subsidy if they applied for admission from outside the state. The second reason is invalid because the challenged statute makes no distinction between established Connecticut residents and new residents who have paid varying amounts of state taxes. The third reason is invalid because the state has other reasonable and practicable means of determining whether Connecticut students are bona fide Connecticut residents.

> We hold only that a permanent irrebuttable presumption of nonresidence—the means adopted by Connecticut to preserve that legitimate interest [of limiting state subsidized education to its residents]—is violative of the Due Process Clause, because it provides no opportunity for students who applied from out of state to demonstrate that they have become bona fide Connecticut residents. The state can establish such reasonable criteria for in-state status as to make virtually certain that students who are not, in fact, bona fide residents of the State, but who have come there solely for educational purposes, cannot take advantage of the in-state rates.

The Court implied in a footnote that Connecticut could constitutionally create a one-year residency requirement for any student seeking resident tuition rates.

U.S. Department of Agriculture v. Murry, 413 U.S. 508 (1973)

Facts: Section 5(b) of the Food Stamp Act of 1964, as amended, renders ineligible for food stamps any household that includes a member over 18 years of age who has been claimed as a tax dependent by a taxpayer who is not eligible for the stamps. The ineligibility lasts both during the tax year in which the dependency was claimed and the following 12 months. A lower federal court ruled in favor of a challenge to the constitutionality of section 5(b) on the ground that its ineligibility provisions were so arbitrary as to violate due process.

Question: Is section 5(b), rendering certain households ineligible for food stamps regardless of need, so arbitrary as to violate due process?

Decision: Yes. Opinion by Justice Douglas. Vote: 5-4.

Reasons: The legislative history of section 5(b) reflects a concern about abuses of the food stamp program by college students who are the children of wealthy parents. Nevertheless, section 5(b) deprives otherwise needy and eligible households of food stamps if it appears that a household member 18 years or older is claimed by someone as a tax dependent. Observing that there was no rational relationship between the need of a household for food stamps and the time during which it was rendered ineligible for stamps by virtue of the "tax dependency" provision of section 5(b), the Court concluded that the assumptions of fact concerning household needs under that section were so arbitrary as to violate due process.

U.S. Department of Agriculture v. Moreno, 413 U.S. 528 (1973)

Facts: Section 3(e) of the Food Stamp Act of 1964, as amended, (Act) which excluded from participation in the food stamp program any household containing an individual unrelated to any other member of the household, was challenged as unconstitutional on the ground that such exclusion was so arbitrary and irrational as to violate due process.

Question: Does the "unrelated person" provision of section 3(e) create an irrational classification of households in violation of due process?

Decision: Yes. Opinion by Justice Brennan. Vote: 7-2.

Reasons: A legislative classification must generally be sustained if rationally related to a legitimate governmental interest. The stated purposes of the Act are to stimulate agricultural purchases and to aid low-income families in meeting their personal nutritional requirements. "The challenged statutory classification (households of related persons versus households containing one or more unrelated persons) is clearly irrelevant to" these purposes. Moreover, the challenged classification is not rationally related to other valid governmental interests such as the prevention of fraud in administering the food stamp program. The legislative history of the unrelated-person provision reveals that it was intended to prevent so-called "hippies" and "hippie communes" from participating in the food stamp program. This purpose cannot sustain the constitutionality of section 3(e) because "a bare desire to harm a politically unpopular group cannot constitute a *legitimate* governmental interest."

Robinson v. Hanrahan, 409 U.S. 38 (1972)

Facts: After Robinson was arrested and was being held in jail on a charge of armed robbery, the state of Illinois instituted forfeiture proceedings against his automobile pursuant to an Illinois statute. Although it knew Robinson was in Cook County jail at the time, the state mailed notice of the pending forfeiture proceedings to his home address. When a state court ordered the forfeiture and sale of the vehicle after an ex parte hearing in which Robinson did not participate, he sued to set the order aside on the ground that he did not receive sufficient notice of the forfeiture proceeding to satisfy due process.

Question: Did Robinson receive sufficient notice of the forfeiture proceedings to satisfy due process of law?

Decision: No. Per curiam opinion. Vote: 9-0.

Reasons: In *Mullane* v. *Central Hanover Bank and Trust Co.,* 339 U.S. 306 (1950), the Court held that "[a]n elementary and fundamental requirement of

11

due process in any proceeding which is to be accorded finality is notice reasonably calculated, under all the circumstances, to apprise interested parties of the pendency of the action and afford them an opportunity to present their objections." Using this standard of due process, the Court specifically held in *Mullane* that notice by publication is not sufficient with respect to an individual whose name and address are known or easily ascertainable. "In the instant case, the State knew that appellant [Robinson] was not at the address to which the notice was mailed and, moreover, knew also that appellant could not get to that address since he was at that very time confined in the Cook County jail. Under these circumstances it cannot be said that the State made any effort to provide notice which was 'reasonably calculated' to apprise appellant of the pendency of the forfeiture proceedings," and thus the notice which Robinson received did not comport with due process.

Gibson v. Berryhill, 411 U.S. 564 (1973)

Facts: The Alabama Optometric Association (Association), a professional organization whose membership was limited to independent practitioners, filed charges before the Alabama Board of Optometry (Board) against various named optometrists, all of whom were duly licensed under Alabama law but were the salaried employees of Lee Optical Company (Company). The Association claimed that the named optometrists, by accepting employment with the Company, had engaged in "unprofessional conduct" and asked the Board to revoke the licenses of the individuals charged after due notice and a proper hearing. Two days later, the Board, whose membership was limited to those in the Association, sued the Company in state court, claiming it was engaged in the unlawful practice of optometry. The individual optometrists charged with unprofessional conduct before the Board then brought suit under 42 U.S. Code, 1983 against the Board and Association in federal court, seeking to enjoin the Board from hearing the pending charges against them on the ground that the Board was biased and could not provide the individuals with a fair and impartial hearing in conformity with due process of law. A three-judge court ruled in favor of the individuals employed by the Company, concluding that the Board was biased, that exhaustion of administrative remedies before the Board was not required because the constitutionality of the Board's composition was challenged, and that notions of comity did not require the federal court to stay its proceedings until the Board's state court suit against the Company terminated.

Question: Did the three-judge district court properly adjudicate the merits of the claim by the individual optometrists?

Decision: Yes. Opinion by Justice White. Vote: 9-0.

Reasons: Because membership on the Board was limited to Association members (all independent optometrists who would profit substantially if the Company-employed optometrists had their licenses revoked), the Board members had a sufficient financial stake in the outcome of the disciplinary charges before them as to constitutionally compel their disqualification from the proceedings.

The Court concluded that the complaining optometrists were not required to exhaust their administrative remedies before the Board, not only because such remedies generally need not be exhausted when section 1983 claims are made but also because it was alleged that the Board provided a constitutionally inadequate administrative remedy.

Regarding the principles of equity, comity, and federalism expressed in *Younger* v. *Harris,* 401 U.S. 37 (1971), and *Samuels* v. *Mackell,* 401 U.S. 66 (1971), which generally require a federal court to defer to pending state court proceedings concerning the same matters, the Court held that such deference to the Board was not required in this case because the Board itself was deemed incompetent to adjudicate the issues pending before it. The notions of comity expressed in *Younger* v. *Harris* presuppose the opportunity of the federal court plaintiffs to raise and to have timely decided by a competent state tribunal the federal issues presented.

Dean v. Gadsden Times Publishing Corporation, 412 U.S. 543 (1973)

Facts: An Alabama statute, providing that an employee excused from work for jury duty shall be paid by his employer the difference between his normal wages and the compensation received for serving as a juror, was challenged as unconstitutional on the ground that it deprived employers of property without due process.

Question: Does the challenged Alabama statute requiring an employer to pay the difference between an employee's regular wages and jury pay unconstitutionally deprive employers of property without due process?

Decision: No. Per curiam opinion. Vote: 9-0.

Reasons: In *Day-Brite Lighting Inc.* v. *Missouri,* 342 U.S. 421 (1952), the Court upheld a state statute making it a misdemeanor for an employer to deduct wages of an employee for four hours when the employee absents himself from his job in order to vote. In *Day-Brite* the employer had contended that the statute took his property in violation of due process, but the Court reasoned that state statutes regulating business must be upheld if they serve the public welfare, including the social, moral, political, economic, or physical well-being of the community. Because the challenged Alabama statute serves the public interest in eliminating any economic penalty for jury service, it must be upheld under the authority of *Day-Brite.*

Frontiero v. Richardson, 411 U.S. 677 (1973)

Facts: Under 37 U.S. Code, 401, 403, and 10 U.S. Code, 1072, a serviceman may claim his wife as a "dependent" without regard to whether she is in fact dependent upon him for any part of her support in order to obtain increased quarters, allowances and medical and dental benefits in the uniformed services.

13

However, a servicewoman, under those statutes, may not claim her husband as a "dependent" unless he is in fact dependent upon her for over one-half of his support. A married female Air Force officer challenged the constitutionality of 37 U.S. Code, 401, 403 and 10 U.S. Code, 1072 on the ground that they discriminated against servicewomen in violation of the Due Process Clause of the Fifth Amendment.

Question: Do the challenged uniformed services benefit statutes unconstitutionally discriminate against servicewomen in creating different standards by which servicemen and servicewomen may claim their spouses as "dependents" for purposes of receiving certain government benefits?

Decision: Yes. Opinion by Justice Brennan. Vote: 8-1.

Reasons: "[S]ex, like race and national origin, is an immutable characteristic determined solely by the accident of birth" and thus "the imposition of special disabilities upon the members of a particular sex because of their sex would seem to violate 'the basic concept of our system that legal burdens should bear some relationship to individual responsibility. . . .' " What differentiates sex from such nonsuspect criteria as "intelligence or physical disability, and aligns it with the recognized suspect criteria, is that the sex characteristic frequently bears no relation to ability to perform or contribute to society. . . . [Thus] classifications based upon sex, like classifications based upon race, alienage, or national origin, are inherently suspect and must therefore be subjected to strict judicial scrutiny." Under the challenged statutes, a servicewoman seeking to obtain housing and medical benefits for her spouse must prove his dependency in fact, whereas no such burden is imposed upon servicemen. Additionally, the statutes operate to deny benefits to a servicewoman providing less than one-half her spouse's support, while at the same time granting such benefits to a serviceman who likewise provides less than one-half of his spouse's support. The differential treatment accorded men and women under these statutes serves no purpose other than mere administrative convenience. Although efficacious administration of governmental programs is not without some importance, it cannot constitutionally justify the differential treatment of men and women under the challenged statutes.

Equal Protection

The Court's most significant equal protection cases were in the fields of education, reapportionment, voting rights, and court fees. The rights of aliens and illegitimate children were also extended under the banner of equal protection.

In a case that could have significantly changed the way in which public school systems are financed, the Court upheld a Texas financing scheme relying in part upon local property taxes which permitted wealthy school districts to spend more per pupil with less tax effort than poor districts were able to do. In a case affecting northern school districts, the Court held that once a finding is made that school authorities have purposely segregated some schools within a district, then all schools within that district should be desegregated unless the authorities demonstrate that the intentional segregation did not affect segregation in other schools. The Court also struck down a Mississippi statute authorizing the lending of textbooks to private schools practicing racial discrimination.

The Court retreated somewhat from its intrusion into the "political thicket" in state reapportionment cases by holding that population variances of up to 10 percent between legislative districts are constitutionally permissible and by permitting a variation of over 16 percent in Virginia where it found special circumstances in the relationship between local and state government. The Court also held that political gerrymandering was not unconstitutional per se but was unconstitutional if done for the purpose of diluting the vote of an ethnic minority.

Stepping back from prior cases extending the one-man, one-vote principle to nearly all elected officials, the Court refused to apply that principle to elections in special water storage districts having limited governmental powers. The Court also upheld a voter residency requirement of 50 days duration for state and local elections after implying last term that 30 days was the constitutional limit.

Noting that he could pay the $50 bankruptcy fee by not smoking or attending movies, the Court rejected the contention made by an indigent that such fee constitutionally deprived him of a right to discharge in voluntary bankruptcy. The Court also upheld a $25 filing fee imposed upon indigents seeking judicial review of administrative determinations in welfare cases.

Laws limiting the rights of aliens to practice law and to enter the civil service were held to violate equal protection. The Court reaffirmed its position that laws discriminating against aliens were "suspect" and subject to close judicial scrutiny.

The rights of illegitimate children have been extended in a series of cases going back to 1968. This term the Court struck down a New Jersey welfare program discriminating against families with illegitimate children.

San Antonio Independent School District v. Rodriguez, 411 U.S. 1 (1973)

Facts: A suit attacking the constitutionality of the Texas system of financing public education on equal protection grounds was brought by Mexican-American parents living in the Edgewood Independent School District (Edgewood), which had a low property tax base. In Texas, approximately 50 percent of all public school funds come from the state, 40 percent from local revenues, and 10 percent from federal sources. The state funds were raised and distributed under the Texas Minimum Foundation School Program in the following manner: State and local contributions were made to a fund earmarked specifically for teacher salaries, operating expenses, and transportation costs, the state supplying 80 percent of the funds from general revenues while school districts were responsible for the remaining 20 percent. Each school district's pay-out share of the fund known as the Local Fund Assignment, was apportioned under a formula designed to reflect each district's relative taxpaying ability. The school district's 20 percent contributions to the state fund were financed out of revenues from local property taxation. Any school district desiring to spend more than its Local Fund Assignment could levy local property taxes for this purpose. Under this system of financing public education, Edgewood, having an assessed property value per pupil of $5,960 and a property tax rate of $1.05 per $100 of assessed property, contributed $26 to the education of each child above its Local Fund Assignment of $222 per pupil. Federal funds added another $108 for a total expenditure of $356 per pupil. Alamo Heights School District (Alamo), in contrast, had assessed property value per pupil exceeding $49,000 and a local tax rate of $.85 per $100 of assessed valuation which yielded $333 per pupil. This amount, added to the $225 per pupil from its Local Fund Assignment and $36 per pupil from federal sources, provided Alamo with $594 per pupil.

Question: Is the Texas system of financing public education, relying in part upon local property taxes, unconstitutional in violation of the Equal Protection Clause because it allegedly discriminates against persons living in school districts with low property values?

Decision: No. Opinion by Justice Powell. Vote: 5-4.

Reasons: The Texas scheme of financing public education passes constitutional muster if it has a rational basis. Prior Supreme Court cases have held that when poor persons are absolutely denied some important public benefit, the reasons for such denial are subject to especially careful scrutiny before the deprivation will be upheld against constitutional attack. In this case, however, Texas has not absolutely deprived any school children of an education and the record indicates all Texas school children receive an adequate education. Moreover, the record fails to show that persons living in Texas in districts with low property values also have low incomes. A recent Connecticut study concluded that it was incorrect to assume that the poorest families in that state in terms of income lived in the poorest districts in terms of property values. "For these two reasons—the absence of any evidence that the financing system discriminates against any definable category of 'poor' people or that it results in the absolute deprivation of education—," the Court concluded that past case law did not require that the Texas financing scheme must satisfy the "compelling state interest" standard in order to be upheld under the Constitution.

The Court also concluded that the mere fact that the complainants asserted a denial of equal education did not alter the general rule that state laws comport with equal protection if they are rational. Prior Supreme Court cases have held that "fundamental" constitutional rights such as the right to be free from racial discrimination and the right of interstate travel may be impinged by state laws only if such laws serve a substantial or compelling state interest. But education is afforded neither explicit nor implicit protection under the Constitution and thus cannot properly be constitutionally characterized as fundamental. "It is not the province of this Court to create substantive constitutional rights in the name of guaranteeing equal protection of the laws."

The challenged Texas scheme of financing has a constitutionally rational purpose. While assuring a basic education for every child in the State, it permits and encourages a large measure of participation in and control of each district's schools at the local level. . . . While it is no doubt true that reliance on local property taxation for school revenues provides less freedom of choice with respect to expenditures for some districts than for others, the existence of "some inequality" in the manner in which the State's rationale is achieved is not alone a sufficient basis for striking down the entire system. . . . The people of Texas may be justified in believing other systems of school finance, which place more of the financial responsibility in the hands of the State, will result in a comparable lessening of desired local autonomy.

The Court thus held that the Texas scheme for financing public education did not violate the Equal Protection Clause and indicated its increasing tendency to leave the resolution of what are commonly viewed as "social problems" to the legislatures. The Court voiced its opposition to judicial legislation in the guise of constitutional interpretation by stating:

In its essential characteristics the Texas plan for financing public education reflects what many educators for a half century have thought was an enlightened approach to a problem for which there is no perfect solution. We are unwilling to assume for ourselves a level of wisdom superior to that of legislators, scholars, and educational authorities in 49 States, especially where the alternatives proposed are only recently conceived and nowhere yet tested.

Keyes v. School District No. 1, Denver, Colorado, 413 U.S. 189 (1973)

Facts: A lower federal court found that the Denver School Board (Board) by use of various techniques such as the manipulation of student attendance zones, school site selection and a neighborhood school policy caused several schools within the entire Denver school district to be segregated. Denver schools had never operated under laws mandating or permitting racial segregation in public education. The plaintiffs, Negroes and Hispanos, unsuccessfully contended that once they had proven that some of the schools within the school system were segregated due to Board action, then they were entitled to a decree directing desegregation of the entire school district.

Question: Once it is determined that a substantial portion of a school district is segregated due to Board policies, must the entire district be desegregated unless the Board proves that its policies did not taint certain schools?

Decision: Yes. Opinion by Justice Brennan. Vote: 7-1.

Reasons: The Court first concluded that the lower court erred in separating Negroes and Hispanos for purposes of defining a "segregated" school. Observing that the Hispano and Negro suffer common economic and cultural deprivation and discrimination, the Court stated the schools with a combined predominance of those ethnic groups should be deemed "segregated" for constitutional purposes.

Regarding the question of the proper scope of the desegregation decree, the Court stated that "where plaintiffs prove that the school authorities have carried out a systematic program of segregation affecting a substantial portion of the students, schools, teachers and facilities within the school system, it is only common sense to conclude that there exists a predicate for a finding of the existence of a dual school system." The Court thus held that once plaintiffs prove that a substantial portion of a school district is segregated due to official action, the entire district must be desegregated absent proof by school authorities that the racial composition of the remaining schools was not affected by the deliberately segregative policies. The Court further held that a finding of "intentionally segregative school board actions in a meaningful portion of a school system . . . creates a presumption that other segregated schooling within the system is not adventitious" and therefore must be corrected.

Norwood v. Harrison, 413 U.S. 455 (1973)

Facts: A Mississippi statute authorizing the lending of textbooks to private schools, whether or not they practiced racial discrimination, was challenged as unconstitutional in violation of the Equal Protection Clause of the Fourteenth Amendment.

Question: Does the lending of textbooks by the state to private schools practicing racial discrimination violate the Equal Protection Clause?

Decision: Yes. Opinion by Chief Justice Burger. Vote: 9-0.

Reasons: Prior case law makes clear that states cannot constitutionally give tuition grants to students attending racially discriminatory private schools. Free textbooks, like tuition grants, give support to racial discrimination practiced by private schools. A state "may not induce, encourage, or promote private persons to accomplish what it is constitutionally forbidden to accomplish."

The Court carefully observed, however, that its decision did not foreclose a state from providing electricity, water, police, and fire protection, general services over which the state generally has a monopoly, to private schools which practice racial discrimination. Textbooks, the Court noted in contrast, are readily available from sources independent of the state and are provided only in connection with schools.

Mahan v. Howell, 410 U.S. 315 (1973)

Facts: A Virginia apportionment statute regarding the election of its 100-member House of Delegates (House) provided for 52 single-member, multimember and floater delegate districts whose per delegate populations varied by as much as 16.4 percent. The 16.4 percent variations in per delegate population of the House districts allegedly resulted from Virginia's desire to follow political subdivision lines in drawing districts because the Virginia state legislature had the power to enact much local legislation. The apportionment statute also provided for 40 single-member senatorial districts containing nearly equal populations.

18

However, the fifth senatorial district was deemed to contain 36,700 naval personnel "homeported" there because that was where they were counted on official census tracts, although in fact only about 8,100 of such personnel lived within the fifth district. Both the Virginia House and Senate reapportionment schemes were attacked in a three-judge district court on the ground that they were unconstitutional in violation of the Equal Protection Clause because the percentage population variations did not comport with the one-person, one-vote principle established by earlier Supreme Court decisions. The district court concluded that the 16.4 percent variation was sufficient to condemn the House reapportionment scheme and devised its own redistricting plan having a population percentage variation of slightly over 10 percent. Regarding the fifth Senate district, deemed to have 36,700 naval personnel, but whose personnel actually were scattered in the fifth, sixth, and seventh Senate districts, the district court concluded that in the absence of more precise population data needed to create three single-member districts more closely representing their actual populations, it would combine those districts into one multimember district.

Questions: Did the district court properly declare the Virginia House reapportionment scheme unconstitutional because it contained differences of up to 16.4 percent between delegate district populations? Did the district court properly revise the Senate reapportionment scheme to include a multimember district because of the uncertain location of naval personnel?

Decision: No to the first question and yes to the second. Opinion by Justice Rehnquist. Vote: 5-3.

Reasons: Prior Supreme Court decisions in *Kirkpatrick* v. *Preisler,* 394 U.S. 526 (1969) and *Wells* v. *Rockefeller,* 394 U.S. 592 (1969) did invalidate state reapportionment statutes for federal congressional districts having maximum population percentage deviations of 5.97 percent and 13.1 percent, respectively. But the Court has always indicated that "more flexibility was constitutionally permissible with respect to state legislative apportionment . . . ." for two reasons: (1) the larger number of seats to be distributed in state legislative bodies may justify the use of political subdivision lines in state reapportionment schemes, and (2) ensuring a voice to political subdivisions in state legislatures when local governmental entities are charged with various responsibilities incident to the operation of state government may justify drawing state legislative district lines to keep political subdivisions intact. Nevertheless, the paramount objective, even in state reapportionment schemes, must be substantial equality of population among the various districts so that the vote of any citizen is approximately equal in weight to that of any other citizen in the state. Virginia, whose state legislature has power to enact local legislation involving political subdivisions, reapportioned its House with a 16.4 percent variation in per delegate district population to provide representation to political subdivisions as subdivisions. Since the 16.4 percent variation was the minimum necessary to achieve the state's rational goal of providing state representation to local subdivisions, and since deviation from the general equal population standard of districting is constitutionally permissible if it serves a rational state interest, the Virginia House reapportionment plan passes constitutional muster. The Court noted that although the 16.4 percent variation "may well approach tolerable [constitutional] limits, we do not believe it exceeds them."

The Court concluded that the district court's combination of the fifth, sixth, and seventh Senate districts into one multimember district to achieve equal population districts per Senate member was proper because the census figures concerning the location of the naval personnel in the fifth district and relied upon by the legislature were clearly erroneous and because any further delay in reapportioning would have seriously disrupted the fall 1971 elections.

Gaffney v. Cummings, 412 U.S. 735 (1973)

Facts: A Connecticut state reapportionment plan for its House of Representatives providing for a maximum deviation of 7.83 percent between the largest and smallest population districts was challenged as unconstitutional on grounds that: (1) it violated the one-man, one-vote principle and thus equal protection, and (2) the districts were drawn to create "safe" Democratic and Republican seats and thereby create representation in the House according to the statewide political strengths of the Democratic and Republican parties. A lower federal court held the reapportionment plan unconstitutional, stating that partisan political structuring could not justify departing from the requirement of population equality among districts.

Questions: Did the challenged state reapportionment plan providing for a 7.83 percent deviation from population equality among districts infringe the one-man, one-vote principle in violation of the Equal Protection Clause? Is it unconstitutional per se for districts to be drawn for partisan political purposes?

Decision: No to both questions. Opinion by Justice White. Vote: 6-3.

Reasons: Although the requirement of Article I, Section 2 of the Constitution that representatives be chosen "by the people of the several States" mandates strict adherence to population equality among congressional districts, state reapportionment schemes are subject to the less demanding requirements of the Equal Protection Clause. "[M]inor deviations from mathematical equality among state legislative districts are insufficient to make out a prima facie case of invidious discrimination under the Fourteenth Amendment so as to require justification by the State." State legislative apportionment schemes achieving fair and effective representation for all citizens pass constitutional muster and the Connecticut plan having a maximum of variation of about 8 percent between the largest and smallest House districts meets this standard.

The Court also rejected the contention that "political gerrymandering" rendered a reapportionment plan per se unconstitutional, noting that "[p]olitics and political considerations are inseparable from districting and apportionment."

Thus, the Court held that the challenged plan was not rendered unconstitutional because it was drawn with the purpose of achieving representation in the House in proportion to the statewide political strengths of the Democratic and Republican parties.

White v. Regester, 412 U.S. 755 (1973)

Facts: A reapportionment plan for the Texas House of Representatives adopted in 1970 was challenged as unconstitutional on the grounds that: (1) the total variation in population between the largest and smallest districts was 9.9 percent and thus in violation of the one-man, one-vote principle, and (2) multi-member districts for two counties were drawn purposefully to dilute the vote of the black and Mexican-American communities. A lower federal court upheld both of these contentions.

Questions: Did the challenged Texas state reapportionment plan with a maximum of 9.9 percent deviation in population between the largest and smallest districts violate the one-man, one-vote principle embodied in the Equal Protection Clause? Were the challenged multimember districts drawn to discriminate against racial minorities and thus in violation of equal protection?

Decision: No to the first question and yes to the second. Opinion by Justice White. Vote: 6-3.

Reasons: "It is plain from *Mahan* v. *Howell,* 410 U.S. 315 (1973), and *Gaffney* v. *Cummings,* 412 U.S. 735 (1973) that state reapportionment statutes are not subject to the same strict standards [of population equality] applicable to reapportionment of congressional seats. . . . [W]e cannot glean an equal protection violation from the single fact that two legislative districts in Texas differ from one another by as much as 9.9 percent. . . . Not every deviation from absolute population equality among state districts has to be justified to satisfy equal protection. The Court observed, however, that differences in population among districts exceeding 9.9 percent would probably not be tolerable without justification "based on legitimate considerations incident to the effectuation of a rational state policy."

The Court affirmed the lower court judgment insofar as it invalidated the two challenged multimember districts and ordered those districts to be drawn into single-member districts. Multimember districts used invidiously to cancel out or minimize the voting strength of racial groups are unconstitutional. To sustain such a contention, racial groups must produce evidence "to support findings that the political processes leading to nomination and election were not equally open to participation by them—that its members had less opportunity than did other residents in the district to participate in the political processes and to elect legislators of their choice." Because both the black and Mexican-American communities had met their burden of proof in this regard, the lower court's invalidation of the two multimember districts must be upheld.

21

Sayler Land Co. v. Tulare Water District, 410 U.S. 719 (1973)

Facts: A water storage district, organized pursuant to California law primarily to acquire, store, and distribute water for farming, was governed by a board of directors who were elected solely by owners of land within the district whose votes were "weighted" according to the assessed valuation of their land. Incidental to its power to plan and execute projects "for the acquisition, appropriation, diversion, storage, conservation, and distribution of water," the water storage district was empowered to acquire and improve projects connected with water drainage, reclamation, and the generation and distribution of hydroelectric power. The water district also fixed tolls and charges for the use of water in proportion to the services and benefits a landowner received. The California statute, limiting the franchise in elections of water storage district directors to landowners and weighting their votes according to the assessed valuation of their lands, was challenged as unconstitutional in violation of the Equal Protection Clause and the one-man, one-vote requirement of *Avery* v. *Midland County,* 390 U.S. 474 (1968) and *Hadley* v. *Junior College District,* 397 U.S. 50 (1970).

Question: Does the method by which California elects directors of water storage districts violate the Equal Protection Clause?

Decision: No. Opinion by Justice Rehnquist. Vote: 6-3.

Reasons: In *Avery* and *Hadley,* the Court applied the one-man, one-vote requirement to elected county government officials and to the election of trustees in a junior college school district but specifically reserved the question of whether such a constitutional requirement would apply to elected directors of "a special-purpose unit of government assigned the performance of functions affecting definable groups of constituents more than other constituents. . . ." In California water storage districts, the costs of projects are assessed against district lands in accordance with the benefits accruing to each tract held in separate ownership, and water tolls and charges are similarly apportioned. Delinquent payment of such charges result in a lien on the owners' land. "There is no way that the economic burdens of district operations can fall on residents *qua* residents, and the operations of the districts primarily affect the land within their boundaries." The Court thus concluded that by reason of its special limited purpose and of the disproportionate effect of its activities on landowners as a group, the water storage district fell within the exception to the one-man, one-vote rule set forth in *Avery* and *Hadley.*

The Court also rejected the contention that limiting the franchise to landowners in proportion to the value of their landholdings in water storage district elections invidiously discriminated against non-landholding residents, lessees, and poor landholders. Excluding residents from voting *qua* residents the Court found was rational because the state might conclude that since landowners as a class were to bear the entire burden of the district's costs then they should be exclusively charged with responsibility for its operation. The Court deemed the exclusion of lessees from voting as rational because: (1) letting short-term lessees vote would lend itself to voting manipulation and complicate the administration of the voting system and, (2) a lessee could contract if he so desired with his lessor to acquire the lessor's right to vote for district directors. Weighting the votes of landowners in proportion to the assessed valuation of their land the Court concluded was rational because both the benefits and burdens caused by the water storage district's acts were also in proportion to the assessed value of each voter's land.

Associated Enterprises, Inc. v. *Toltec Watershed Improvement District,* 410 U.S. 743 (1973)

Facts: A Wyoming statute authorizing the establishment of a watershed improvement district in a referendum in which only landowners within the district were entitled to vote and whose votes were weighted according to acreage was challenged as unconstitutional under the Equal Protection Clause.

Question: Does the Wyoming limitation on voting to create watershed improvement districts violate equal protection?

Decision: No. Per curiam opinion. Vote: 6-3.

Reasons: In *Sayler Land Company* v. *Tulare Water District,* 410 U.S. 719 (1973), the Court upheld the constitutionality of a California law limiting the voting for water storage district directors to district landowners whose votes were weighted in proportion to the assessed valuation of their land.

> Like the California water storage district, the Wyoming watershed district is a governmental unit of special or limited purpose whose activities have a disproportionate effect on landowners within the district. The district's operations are conducted through projects and the land is assessed for any benefits received. . . . Such assessments constitute a lien on the land until paid. As in *Sayler* . . . we hold that the State could rationally conclude that landowners are primarily burdened and benefited by the establishment and operation of watershed districts and that it may condition the vote accordingly.

Marston v. *Lewis,* 410 U.S. 679 (1973)

Facts: Arizona's requirement of a 50-day residence in the state as a prerequisite for voting in state and local elections was challenged as unconstitutional because it allegedly penalized the exercise of the constitutional right of interstate travel. Arizona contended the 50-day period was needed to prevent fraud and errors in preparing registration lists and to maintain its volunteer deputy registrar system which operated without large staffs.

Question: Is Arizona's 50-day residency requirement for voting in state and local elections unconstitutional?

Decision: No. Per curiam opinion. Vote: 6-3.

Reasons: In *Dunn* v. *Blumstein,* 405 U.S. 330 (1972), the Court struck down Tennessee's voter residency requirement of one year in the state and three months in the county as a condition to voting in state and local elections. The Court noted in *Dunn* "that 30 days appears to be an ample period of time for the State to complete whatever administrative tasks are necessary to prevent fraud. . . . In the present case, we are confronted with a recent and amply justifiable legislative judgment that 50 days rather than 30 days is necessary to promote the State's important interest in accurate voter lists. The Constitution is not so rigid that that determination and others like it may not stand."

Rosario v. Rockefeller, 410 U.S. 752 (1973)

Facts: Under the New York election law, a voter must enroll in the party of his choice at least 30 days before the general election in November in order to vote in the next subsequent party primary. (Exemptions from this requirement were allowed to persons attaining voting age after the last general election and to certain other classes of voters.) The cutoff date for enrollment occurred approximately eight months prior to a presidential primary and 11 months prior to a non-presidential primary. New York residents challenged the constitutionality of this party registration requirement on the ground that it operated to exclude newly registered voters from participating in the primary election of the party of their choice in violation of the Equal Protection Clause.

Question: Does the New York election law requiring as a condition to participation in a party primary election that a voter enroll in the party 30 days prior to the last general election violate equal protection by invidiously discriminating against those voters failing to meet the deadline?

Decision: No. Opinion by Justice Stewart. Vote: 5-4.

Reasons: Past Supreme Court decisions have held that a state may totally deny the electoral franchise to a particular class of residents only if justified by a "compelling state interest." In this case, the challenged election law did not absolutely disenfranchise any class of voters by imposing a time deadline on voter enrollment to participate in party primary elections. Any disenfranchisement from voting in primary elections is caused solely by a voter's failure to take timely steps to effect his party enrollment. The only constitutional question in this case is whether the time limitation imposed by the challenged election law imposes an unconstitutionally onerous burden on voting and freedom of political association by requiring voters to choose party affiliation eight or eleven months in advance of primary elections "before prospective voters have knowledge of the candidates or issues to be involved in the next primary elections." The purpose of the time limitation is "to inhibit party 'raiding' whereby voters in sympathy with one party designate themselves as voters of another party so as to influence or determine the results of the other party's primary. . . ." To allow enrollment any time after the general election would not have the same deterrent effect on raiding as the 30 day pre-general election requirement for enrollment because it would not put the voter in the unseemly position of asking to be enrolled in one party while at the same time intending to vote immediately for another. Reasoning that preservation of the integrity of the electoral process is a legitimate state goal and that the time limitation provision in the challenged election law furthered that interest by discouraging party raiding in primary elections, the Court held that the challenged election law was rational and thus passed constitutional muster under the Equal Protection Clause.

Gomez v. Perez, 409 U.S. 535 (1973)

Facts: An illegitimate child challenged the Texas law granting legitimate children a judicially enforceable right of support from their natural fathers while denying that right to illegitimate children on the ground that it denied illegitimate children equal protection of the laws.

Question: Does the Texas child support law invidiously discriminate against illegitimate children in violation of the Equal Protection Clause of the Fourteenth Amendment?

Decision: Yes. Per curiam opinion. Vote: 7-2.

Reasons: In *Levy* v. *Louisiana,* 391 U.S. 68 (1968), the Court held that under the Equal Protection Clause a state may not generally give children a right of action for the wrongful death of their parents but deny such a right to illegitimate children. In *Weber* v. *Aetna Casualty & Surety Co.,* 406 U.S. 164 (1972), the Court held that unacknowledged illegitimate children could not constitutionally be excluded from sharing equally with other children in the recovery of workmen's compensation benefits available because of the death of a parent. "Under these decisions a State may not invidiously discriminate against illegitimate children by denying them substantial benefits accorded children generally." The Court thus held that "once a State posits a judicially enforceable right on behalf of children to needed support from their natural fathers there is no constitutionally sufficient justification for denying such an essential right to a child simply because her natural father has not married her mother."

New Jersey Welfare Rights Organization v. Cahill, 411 U.S. 619 (1973)

Facts: The New Jersey "Assistance to Families of the Working Poor" program, which limited benefits to only those otherwise qualified families comprised of married couples having at least one minor child of both, the natural child of one adopted by the other, or a child adopted by both, was challenged as invidiously discriminatory against illegitimate children and thus unconstitutional in violation of the Equal Protection Clause.

Question: Does the New Jersey "Working Poor" program invidiously discriminate against illegitimate children in violation of equal protection?

Decision: Yes. Per curiam opinion. Vote: 7-2.

Reasons: "[A]lthough the challenged classification turns upon the marital status of the parents, as well as upon the child-parent relationship, in practical effect it operates almost invariably to deny benefits to illegitimate children while granting benefits to those children who are legitimate." Prior Supreme Court cases in *Weber* v. *Aetna Casualty & Surety Co.,* 406 U.S. 164 (1972), *Levy* v. *Louisiana,* 391 U.S. 68 (1968) and *Gomez* v. *Perez,* 409 U.S. 535 (1973) held that states may not exclude illegitimate children from sharing equally with other children in the recovery of workmen's compensation benefits for the death of a parent, may not create a right of action in favor of children for the wrongful death of a parent and exclude illegitimate children from the benefit of such a right, and may not deny to illegitimate children the same enforceable right of support against a natural father given to legitimate children. The reasoning behind these cases was that it is illogical and unjust to impose legal disabilities upon illegitimate children who have no responsibility for, or control over, their status. Because the benefits extended under the challenged New Jersey program are indispensable to the health of both legitimate and illegitimate children, denying the benefits to illegitimate children, allegedly to preserve and strengthen family life, violates the Equal Protection Clause under the *Weber, Levy* and *Gomez* line of decisions.

Sugarman v. Dougall, 413 U.S. 634 (1973)

Facts: A New York civil service statute excluding aliens from appointment to any position in the competitive class was successfully challenged in lower federal court as unconstitutional in violation of the Equal Protection Clause.

Question: Does the challenged New York civil service statute unjustly discriminate against aliens in violation of equal protection?

Decision: Yes. Opinion by Justice Blackmun. Vote: 8-1.

Reasons: Aliens as a class are a prime example of a discrete and insular minority and thus statutory classifications based upon alienage are subject to close judicial scrutiny. The challenged New York statute is neither narrowly confined nor precise in its application. Its ineligibility restrictions may apply to sanitation employees as well as to policy makers. Moreover, no citizenship requirement is imposed upon persons holding elective and high appointive offices. Thus, the statute does not withstand close judicial scrutiny.

The Court added, however, that its decision did not prevent a state from refusing to hire aliens on an individualized basis nor require citizenship as a qualification for office in an appropriately defined class of positions.

In re Griffiths, 413 U.S. 717 (1973)

Facts: A Connecticut rule restricting the practice of law to United States citizens was attacked on the ground that it unconstitutionally discriminated against resident aliens in violation of equal protection.

Question: Does the exclusion of aliens from the Connecticut bar violate the Equal Protection Clause of the Fourteenth Amendment?

Decision: Yes. Opinion by Justice Powell. Vote: 7-2.

Reasons: Laws discriminating against aliens pass constitutional muster only if the state sustains its burden of showing that "its purpose or interest is both constitutionally permissible and substantial, and that its use of the [discrimination] is 'necessary to the accomplishment' of its purpose or the safeguarding of its interest." States have a constitutionally permissible and substantial interest in requiring all applicants to the bar to be of high moral and professional character. That interest, however, can be achieved by scrutinizing applicants on a case-by-case basis, requiring tests of competence and oaths of loyalty, and providing sanctions against unprofessional conduct. In this case, Connecticut has "not established that it must exclude all aliens from the practice of law in order to vindicate its undoubted interest in high professional standards."

United States v. Kras, 409 U.S. 434 (1973)

Facts: As a condition to a discharge in voluntary bankruptcy, the Bankruptcy Act imposes a $50 filing fee which goes toward paying the referees' salary and expense fund and toward compensating trustees and clerks, thereby making the administration of bankruptcy self-supporting. In cases of voluntary bankruptcy, the fees may be paid in installments over a nine-month period ($1.28 weekly). Kras filed a voluntary petition in bankruptcy, seeking to have some $6,500 in debts discharged, and moved to proceed without paying the $50 filing fee because of his poverty. In support of his motion, Kras submitted an uncontradicted affidavit stating that he had a household of five persons, one suffering from cystic fibrosis; that he was unemployed and had unsuccessfully sought steady employment; and that his household lived on $366 of public assistance per month. The district court granted Kras's motion, permitting him to receive a discharge in bankruptcy without paying the statutory filing fee, on the ground that the filing fee statute violated Kras's right of due process and equal protection.

Question: Does the bankruptcy statute requiring a $50 filing fee as a condition to receiving a discharge in voluntary bankruptcy deny Kras due process or equal protection?

Decision: No. Opinion by Justice Blackmun. Vote: 5-4.

Reasons: In *Boddie v. Connecticut,* 401 U.S. 371 (1971), the Court held a Connecticut statute (which imposed a $60 court fee as a condition for getting a divorce) unconstitutional as applied to indigents because it effectively operated to deny them an opportunity to be heard in the courts in violation of due process. In reaching this conclusion, the Court in *Boddie* emphasized that the state monopolized the only means of legally dissolving marriage and that imposing a court fee on indigents effectively prevented them from exercising their sensitive and personal right to divorce and remarriage. The Court distinguished the *Kras* case from *Boddie* essentially on two grounds: (1) Kras's inability to get a voluntary discharge in bankruptcy did not affect sensitive personal freedoms as in

Boddie, and (2) Kras had other means of discharging his debts so that court access was not his exclusive remedy. The Court thus concluded that the challenged $50 filing fee did not deny Kras due process.

Turning to the equal protection claim, the Court stated that the challenged statute would pass constitutional muster if it had a rational basis. The Court found this rational basis in the congressional desire to make the bankruptcy system "self-sustaining and paid for by those who use it rather than by tax revenues drawn from the public at large." The Court further observed that the statutory provision permitted the $50 filing fee to be paid over nine months, in weekly installments of $1.28, "less than the price of a movie and little more than the cost of a pack or two of cigarettes."

Ortwein v. Schwab, 410 U.S. 656 (1973)

Facts: Welfare recipients, as permitted by Oregon law, sought judicial review of an administrative decision of the Public Welfare Division which disallowed them certain welfare payments. However, Oregon required that all appellants in civil cases pay a $25 filing fee. Alleging indigency, the welfare recipients challenged the constitutionality of the filing fee requirement on the ground that it invidiously discriminated against the poor in violation of equal protection and due process.

Question: Does imposing a $25 filing fee requirement on indigents seeking judicial review of administrative welfare determinations after an administrative hearing violate equal protection or due process?

Decision: No. Per curiam opinion. Vote: 5-4.

Reasons: "In *United States* v. *Kras,* 409 U.S. 434 (1972), the Court upheld statutorily imposed bankruptcy filing fees as applied to indigents against a claim that such fees denied indigents access to the courts in violation of due process." *Kras* was distinguishable from *Boddie* v. *Connecticut,* 401 U.S. 371 (1971), which struck down on due process grounds court fees as assessed against indigents seeking divorce, largely on the ground that "one's interest in a bankruptcy discharge does not rise to the same constitutional level as one's inability to dissolve his marriage except through the courts." The reasoning of *Kras* governs this case. The interest in receiving welfare is less fundamental than the interest in receiving a divorce. Moreover, the welfare recipients are entitled to an evidentiary administrative determination of their claims unconditioned on the payment of any fee. Under these circumstances, imposing a $25 filing fee on recipients seeking judicial review of their welfare claims does not violate due process.

Regarding the equal protection claims, the Court found a rational basis for the $25 fee in Oregon's desire to defray the costs of operating its court system and thus upheld the fee over the contention that it unconstitutionally discriminated against the poor. Although Oregon waived the fee in certain cases involving habeas corpus, civil commitment, and parental rights, the Court concluded that

28

giving special rights to persons involved in such cases concerning sensitive personal rights, but not to other civil litigants, was not so arbitrary or capricious as to deny equal protection.

Lehnhausen v. *Lake Shore Auto Parts Co.,* 410 U.S. 356 (1973)

Facts: A corporation challenged a 1970 Illinois constitutional amendment which prohibited imposing ad valorem personal property taxes on individuals while permitting such taxes to be levied against corporations and similar entities on the ground that it violated the Equal Protection Clause of the Fourteenth Amendment.

Question: Does the challenged Illinois constitutional amendment exempting only individuals from paying personal property taxes violate equal protection?

Decision: No. Opinion by Justice Douglas. Vote: 9-0.

Reasons: "Where taxation is concerned and no specific right apart from equal protection is imperiled, the States have large leeway in making classifications and drawing lines which in their judgment produce reasonable systems of taxation." After reviewing earlier decisions in which it, *inter alia*, upheld against equal protection challenge a state statute imposing back taxes on land owned by corporations but not individuals and a state excise tax imposed on utilities but not on other business units, the Court concluded, "in the present case . . . making corporations and other like entities liable for ad valorem taxes on personal property but not individuals does not transcend the requirements of equal protection." The Court found a rational basis in the challenged Illinois constitutional provision because in prior use the individual personal property tax proved impossible to administer fairly while the corporate personal property tax was uniformly enforceable.

First Amendment Rights

The Court's important work in the First Amendment area concerned obscenity laws, state aid to nonpublic schools, freedom of speech and of the press, and political rights of government employees.

Regarding obscenity, the Court discarded a 1966 definition of obscene material and concluded the following in a series of cases generally giving legislatures more power to restrict sexually oriented expression and materials: (1) the Twenty-first Amendment gives states the power to prohibit sexually oriented conduct in connection with the sale of liquor even though it is not obscene, (2) words may be constitutionally obscene, (3) obscene material does not acquire immunity from regulation simply because exhibited only to consenting adults, (4) Congress may constitutionally prohibit the importation and interstate transportation of obscene material for private use, (5) expert testimony is unnecessary to prove obscenity, (6) obscenity can constitutionally be determined pursuant to local standards, and (7) the three-pronged constitutional test of obscenity is

29

whether the work, taken as a whole, appeals to the prurient interest, describes or depicts specific sexual conduct in a patently offensive way, and lacks serious literary, artistic, political, or scientific value.

In three cases concerning state reimbursement of nonpublic schools for services and state aid to parents sending their children to nonpublic schools, the Court struck down all the challenged programs under the Establishment Clause, finding that those programs had a primary effect of advancing religion. The 6-3 vote of the Court in these cases seems to indicate that no substantial aid to nonpublic schools, whether in the form of tax credits to parents or otherwise, will pass constitutional muster. In another case, however, the Court upheld limited state aid to a Baptist college in connection with borrowing money. The Court seems disposed to allow more state aid and involvement with religiously affiliated colleges and universities than with parochial elementary and secondary schools at least in part on the belief that religion is not so pervasive at institutions of higher education.

Both federal and state laws prohibiting certain political activity by government employees were upheld against the contention that such laws were unconstitutionally vague and overbroad.

In a significant case for political groups, the Court upheld the rights of broadcasters to refuse as a general policy to sell time for comment on public issues. The Court also upheld the power of states to forbid newspapers to carry "help-wanted" advertisements in sex-designated columns and to place a prior restraint on such advertisements. The dissenters argued that the First Amendment forbade any sanctions against a "violating" newspaper until after its publication.

California v. LaRue, 409 U.S. 109 (1972)

Facts: When the California Department of Alcoholic Beverage Control (Department) promulgated regulations prohibiting certain types of sexual conduct and display in establishments holding liquor licenses issued by the Department, various liquor licensees and "dancers" sued to prohibit the enforcement of such regulations on the ground that they unconstitutionally abridged their freedom of expression guaranteed to them by the First and Fourteenth Amendments.

Question: Do the Department's regulations, which admittedly prohibit conduct not constitutionally obscene, violate the First Amendment in light of the state's authority to regulate the sale of liquor under the Twenty-first Amendment which provides that the "transportation or importation into any State . . . of intoxicating liquors . . ." in violation of that state's laws is prohibited?

Decision: No. Opinion by Justice Rehnquist. Vote: 6-3.

Reasons: "The state regulations here challenged come to us not in the context of censoring a dramatic performance in a theater, but rather in a context of licensing bars and nightclubs to sell liquor by the drink. . . . [T]he broad sweep of the Twenty-first Amendment has been recognized as conferring something more than the normal state authority over public health, welfare, and morals." The

30

Department promulgated the challenged regulations only after hearing testimony to the effect that the type of sexual conduct prohibited by the regulations on premises where liquor is sold may tend to increase sexual offenses. Although agreeing that some of the challenged regulations forbade conduct not legally obscene under the standards set forth in the Court's landmark decision of *Roth* v. *United States,* 354 U.S. 476 (1957), the Court reasoned that these regulations were constitutional both because the Twenty-first Amendment gave the states broad power to regulate the sale of liquor and because the Department's conclusion "that certain sexual performances and the dispensation of liquor by the drink ought not to occur simultaneously at premises which have licenses was not an irrational one."

The Court concluded by noting that "we would poorly serve both the interests for which the State may validly seek vindication and the interests protected by the First and Fourteenth Amendments were we to insist that the sort of Bacchanalian revelries which the Department sought to prevent by these liquor regulations were the constitutional equivalent of a performance by a scantily clad ballet troupe in a theater."

Miller v. California, 413 U.S. 15 (1973)

Facts: The defendant, convicted of violating a California obscenity statute by causing five unsolicited advertising brochures to be sent through the mail, challenged the constitutionality of his conviction on the ground that the jury had been erroneously instructed to evaluate the obscenity of the materials by the contemporary community standards of California rather than of the nation. (In *Memoirs* v. *Massachusetts,* 383 U.S. 413 (1966), the Court stated that for materials to be deemed constitutionally obscene, it must be established that (a) the dominant theme of the material taken as a whole appeals to a prurient interest in sex, (b) the material is patently offensive because it affronts contemporary community standards relating to the description or representation of sexual matters, and (c) the material is utterly without redeeming social value.)

Question: Did the trial judge constitutionally err by instructing the jury to evaluate the obscenity of materials by the contemporary community standards of California?

Decision: No. Opinion by Chief Justice Burger. Vote: 5-4.

Reasons: Before deciding the question, the Court established a new constitutional definition of obscenity after concluding that the three-pronged test established in *Memoirs* had proved unworkable. Noting that obscene material is unprotected by the First Amendment, the Court nevertheless concluded that the inherent dangers in regulating any form of expression required that such regulation be confined to works which "depict or describe sexual conduct" as " specifically defined by the applicable state law. . . ." Accordingly, the Court set forth a new three-pronged test of obscenity: "(a) whether 'the average person applying contemporary community standards' would find that work, taken as a whole, appeals to the prurient in-

31

terest . . ., (b) whether the work depicts or describes, in a patently offensive way, sexual conduct specifically defined by the applicable state law, and (c) whether the work, taken as a whole, lacks serious literary, artistic, political, or scientific value." The Court abandoned the "utterly without redeeming social value" test of *Memoirs,* noting that such test required the prosecution to prove a negative—a burden virtually impossible to meet under criminal standards of proof. Concerning the test of obscenity in (b), the Court gave the following two examples of materials legislatures could proscribe: "(a) Patently offensive representations or descriptions of ultimate sexual acts, normal or perverted, actual or simulated; (b) Patently offensive representations or descriptions of masturbation, excretory functions, and lewd exhibition of the genitals."

Turning to the question of whether local rather than national standards could constitutionally be used to determine whether material appealed to the prurient interest, the Court reasoned that lay jurors could not realistically be expected to determine nor could the state prove the existence of an abstract national standard. Accordingly, the Court held that state community standards could constitutionally be used in determining whether materials are obscene.

Paris Adult Theatre I v. Slaton, 413 U.S. 49 (1973)

Facts: In a state civil proceeding to determine whether certain movie films were obscene and should thus be enjoined under state law from exhibition in a commercial theatre, a state court concluded, assuming the films were obscene, that they were constitutionally protected from suppression if displayed in a commercial theatre with requisite notice to the public of their nature and with reasonable precautions to avoid exposure of the films to minors.

Question: Do otherwise obscene films acquire constitutional immunity from state regulation simply because they are exhibited only to consenting adults?

Decision: No. Opinion by Chief Justice Burger. Vote: 5-4.

Reasons: Although states may have a special interest in regulating the exposure of obscene materials to juveniles and unconsenting adults, states also have legitimate interests in prohibiting commercialized obscenity in order to enhance the quality of life, the community and commercial environment, and perhaps the public safety. Rejecting the contention that state regulation of obscenity was impermissible in the absence of scientific data conclusively proving its harm to persons or society, the Court concluded that states might reasonably determine that a connection between exposure to obscene materials and anti-social behavior existed and constitutionally act upon that determination even though no empirical data conclusively supported it.

The Court also rejected the argument that prohibiting the exposure of obscene materials to consenting adults in a commercial setting violated a constitutional right of privacy under *Stanley* v. *Georgia,* 394 U.S. 557 (1969). In *Stanley,* the Court held that the constitutional right of privacy protected a person from prosecution for possessing obscene materials in his home. Reasoning that commercial settings carry with them no reasonable expectations of privacy, the Court concluded that forbidding the exposure of obscene material to consenting adults in places of public accommodation did not invade any constitutionally protected zone of privacy.

Lastly, the Court observed that expert testimony was not constitutionally required to prove that the challenged films were obscene.

United States v. 12 200-Ft. Reels of Super 8mm Film, 413 U.S. 123 (1973)

Facts: Certain imported obscene materials intended only for private, personal use and possession were seized by customs officers and subjected to a forfeiture action under federal law. The claimant of the obscene materials successfully claimed in a lower federal court that to prohibit the importation of obscene material intended only for private, personal use and possession violated his constitutional right of privacy.

Question: May the United States constitutionally prohibit importation of obscene material which the importer claims is for private, personal use and possession only?

Decision: Yes. Opinion by Chief Justice Burger. Vote: 5-4.

Reasons: Congress has plenary power to regulate imports under Article I, Section 8 of the Constitution, which includes the power to prohibit the introduction of foreign articles. *Stanley v. Georgia,* 394 U.S. 557 (1969), which held that a person has a constitutional right to possess obscene material in the privacy of the home, does not control this case. *Stanley* turned on the right of privacy in the home, and does not permit one to go abroad and bring obscene material into the country for private purposes.

United States v. Orito, 413 U.S. 139 (1973)

Facts: The defendant, charged with knowingly transporting obscene materials in interstate commerce in violation of a federal statute, successfully challenged the constitutionality of that statute in a lower federal court on the ground that it violated the constitutional right of privacy in forbidding the transportation of obscene materials by private carriage or for private use.

Question: Does the challenged federal obscenity statute violate a constitutional right of privacy?

Decision: No. Opinion by Chief Justice Burger. Vote: 5-4.

Reasons: United States v. Thirty-seven Photographs, 402 U.S. 363 (1971) and *United States v. Reidel,* 402 U.S. 351 (1971) foreclose any contention that "some zone of constitutionally protected privacy follows [obscene] materials when they are moved outside the home. . . ."

Regarding the contention that forbidding private transport of obscene materials was unconstitutional, the Court noted that Congress might reasonably conclude such regulation was necessary to prevent any possible exposure to juveniles or to the public generally. "Congress may impose relevant conditions and requirements on those who use the channels of interstate commerce in order that those channels will not become the means of promoting or spreading evil, whether of a physical, moral or economic nature."

Kaplan v. California, 413 U.S. 115 (1973)

Facts: An adult bookstore owner, convicted of selling an obscene book under California law, challenged the constitutionality of that law on the ground that the First Amendment absolutely forbids the suppression of words under obscenity laws.

Question: Can expression by words alone be deemed legally obscene and thus unprotected by the First Amendment?

Decision: Yes. Opinion by Chief Justice Burger. Vote: 5-4.

Reasons: Obscene books have a tendency to circulate among the impressionable young, and a state might reasonably conclude that obscene books encourage or cause antisocial behavior among the young and others. "States need not wait until behavioral experts or educators can provide empirical data [supporting that conclusion] before enacting controls of commerce in obscene materials. . . ."

Papish v. University of Missouri Board of Curators, 410 U.S. 667 (1973)

Facts: Papish, a graduate student in the University of Missouri School of Journalism, was expelled for distributing on campus a newspaper containing both a political cartoon depicting policemen raping the Statue of Liberty and the Goddess of Justice and an article entitled "M--- f--- Acquitted," which discussed the trial and acquittal on an assault charge of a New York City youth who was a member of an organization known as "Up Against the Wall, M--- f---." After exhausting her administrative remedies within the university, Papish brought suit contending that her dismissal was unconstitutional because premised on activities protected by the First Amendment.

Question: Did the university's expulsion of Papish because of her distribution of the offensive newspaper violate her First Amendment right of free speech?

Decision: Yes. Per curiam opinion. Vote: 6-3.

Reasons: Recent precedents in the Supreme Court make clear that neither the political cartoon nor the headline story in this case can be labelled as constitutionally obscene or otherwise unprotected by the First Amendment. The record in this case shows Papish was dismissed solely because of the disapproved content of the newspaper rather than the time, place, or manner of its distribution. "Since the First Amendment leaves no room for the operation of a dual standard in the academic community with respect to the content of speech, and because the state University's action here cannot be justified as a nondiscriminatory application of reasonable rules governing conduct," Papish must be reinstated as a graduate student because a state may not penalize the exercise of First Amendment rights.

Committee for Public Education and Religious Liberty v. Nyquist, 413 U.S. 756 (1973)

Facts: A New York law providing financial assistance to nonpublic elementary and secondary schools was challenged as unconstitutional in violation of the Establishment Clause. The challenged law provided: (a) direct money grants from the state to qualifying nonpublic schools to be used for the maintenance and repair of school facilities, (b) tuition reimbursements ranging from $50-$100 per pupil to low-income parents of children attending elementary or secondary nonpublic schools, and (c) certain income tax benefits to parents whose children were attending elementary or secondary nonpublic schools and whose income was less than $25,000.

Question: Do all three methods under the challenged New York law for providing financial assistance to nonpublic elementary and secondary schools violate the Establishment Clause?

Decision: Yes. Opinion by Justice Powell. Vote: 6-3.

Reasons: Prior decisions "dictate that to pass muster under the Establishment Clause the law in question, first, must reflect a clearly secular legislative purpose, . . . second, must have a primary effect that neither advances nor inhibits religion, . . . and, third, must avoid excessive government entanglement with religion. . . ." All three challenged methods of state aid to nonpublic elementary and secondary schools reflect secular legislative purposes: to preserve a healthy and safe educational environment for all of the state's school children, to promote pluralism and diversity among the state's public and nonpublic schools, and to prevent an already overburdened public school system from the increased burdens resulting from children leaving nonpublic schools for public schools. However, all three methods of state aid to nonpublic elementary and secondary schools have a primary effect that advances religion and thus are unconstitutional. Nearly 85 percent of the nonpublic schools benefiting from state aid under the challenged law are church-related. The "maintenance and repair" grants under that law are not restricted for use in connection with the upkeep of facilities related exclusively for secular purposes. Thus, such grants have a "primary effect that advances religion in that [they] subsidize directly the religious activities of sectarian elementary and secondary schools. . . . New York's tuition reimbursement program also fails the 'effect' test, for much the same reasons that govern its maintenance and repair grants." The unrestricted grants of $50 to $100 per pupil could not constitutionally be given directly to sectarian schools because they clearly would advance religion. The fact that the grants are made to parents makes no difference under the Constitution because "the effect of the aid is unmistakably to provide desired financial support for nonpublic, sectarian institutions." The income tax benefit scheme was also held unconstitutional on the ground that it, like the tuition reimbursement program, had a primary effect that advanced the sectarian activities of religious schools. The Court further observed that the state program of financial assistance to sectarian schools in this case carried grave potential for continuing political strife over aid to religion, something the Establishment Clause was designed to avoid.

Levitt v. Committee for Public Education and Religious Liberty, 413 U.S. 472 (1973)

Facts: A New York law, reimbursing private schools throughout the state for performing various testing and record-keeping services mandated by the state, was challenged as unconstitutional in violation of the Establishment Clause of the First Amendment.

Question: Does the challenged New York law violate the Establishment Clause of the First Amendment?

Decision: Yes. Opinion by Chief Justice Burger. Vote: 8-1.

Reasons: When statutes are challenged as violating the Establishment Clause, the essential inquiry is "whether the challenged state aid has the primary purpose or effect of advancing religion or religious education or whether it leads to excessive entanglement by the State in the affairs of the religious institution." In *Committee for Public Education and Religious Liberty* v. *Nyquist,* 413 U.S. 756 (1973), the Court struck down a New York law authorizing state reimbursement to certain nonpublic schools for the costs of maintenance and repair of school facilities, reasoning that no attempt was made to restrict expenditures related to the upkeep of facilities used exclusively for secular purposes and thus concluding that the statute had the primary effect of advancing religion. In this case, the statute makes no attempt to limit reimbursement to those testing services or examinations that are internally free of religious instruction. "We cannot ignore the substantial risk that these examinations, prepared by teachers under the authority of religious institutions, will be drafted with an eye, unconsciously or otherwise, to inculcate students in the religious precepts of the sponsoring church." The Court thus concluded under the authority of *Nyquist* that the challenged statute had the primary effect of advancing religion and thus violated the Establishment Clause. The contention that the state should be permitted to pay for any school activity mandated by state law was explicitly rejected.

Sloan v. Lemon, 413 U.S. 825 (1973)

Facts: A Pennsylvania statute providing state reimbursement of up to $150 per child to qualifying parents who pay tuition for their children to attend the state's nonpublic elementary and secondary schools was challenged as unconstitutional in violation of the Establishment Clause.

Question: Does the Pennsylvania tuition reimbursement program violate the Establishment Clause?

Decision: Yes. Opinion by Justice Powell. Vote: 6-3.

Reasons: The challenged Pennsylvania program is no different in substance from the New York tuition reimbursement scheme struck down in *Committee for Public Education and Religious Liberty* v. *Nyquist,* 413 U.S. 756 (1973) because a primary effect of the scheme was to advance religion. More than 90 percent of the children attending nonpublic schools in Pennsylvania are enrolled in schools controlled by religious organizations. The state has singled out the parents of these children for a special economic benefit. "Whether that benefit be viewed as a simple tuition subsidy, as an incentive to parents to send their children to sectarian schools, or as a reward for having done so, at bottom its intended consequence is to preserve and support religion-oriented institutions." Thus, the Pennsylvania tuition grant scheme violates the constitutional mandate against state sponsorship or financial support of religion or religious institutions.

Lemon v. Kurtzman, 411 U.S. 193 (1973)

Facts: On June 28, 1971, the Supreme Court held that a Pennsylvania statutory program to reimburse nonpublic sectarian schools for certain secular purposes violated the Establishment Clause of the First Amendment and remanded the case to a three-judge district court for further proceedings consistent with its opinion in *Lemon* v. *Kurtzman,* 403 U.S. 602 (1971) *(Lemon I).* On remand, the district court enjoined the state from reimbursing nonpublic sectarian schools for educational services performed after June 28, 1971. The successful plaintiffs in *Lemon I* subsequently sued to enjoin the payment of some $24 million set aside by Pennsylvania to compensate nonpublic sectarian schools for educational services rendered by them during the 1970-71 school year. The challenge was based on the contention that to permit such reimbursement would violate the Establishment Clause.

Question: Can Pennsylvania constitutionally pay $24 million to nonpublic sectarian schools for educational services rendered prior to *Lemon I?*

Decision: Yes. Opinion by Chief Justice Burger. Vote: 5-3.

Reasons: In *Lemon I,* the Court concluded that the Pennsylvania auditing scheme designed to restrict state payments to nonpublic sectarian schools to secular rather than sectarian services fostered an "excessive entanglement" with religion, and thus the statutory reimbursement program violated the Establishment Clause. The Court found it unnecessary to decide in *Lemon I* whether the challenged statute had the "primary effect" of promoting the cause of religion in contravention of the Constitution. In this case the plaintiffs did not challenge until August 1971 the constitutionality of the state's reimbursement to church-related schools for certain secular educational services provided during the 1970-71 school year. The Court reasoned that in these circumstances permitting the one-time distribution of state funds to Pennsylvania's nonpublic schools would not substantially undermine the constitutional interests at stake in *Lemon I.* Payment of the disputed sums would compel no further oversight of the instructional processes of sectarian schools and would leave no potential for divisive political conflict.

A final audit would involve a ministerial balancing of expenditures and receipts and minimal contact of the state with the affairs of sectarian schools.

The Court also rejected the contention that the single-time state payment of $24 million to sectarian schools had the primary effect of promoting religion in violation of the Establishment Clause. Stating that the Court's holding in *Lemon I* was not clearly foreshadowed by prior decisions, that the plaintiffs were dilatory in opposing the $24 million reimbursement, and that the $24 million sum reflected no more than the sectarian schools' reliance on promised payment for expenses incurred by them prior to June 28, 1971, the Court concluded that Pennsylvania's challenged payments to sectarian schools for secular services performed prior to *Lemon I* were constitutionally permissible. The Court noted that on the facts of this case the constitutionality of the $24 million single-time payment "must be measured in the totality of circumstances and in light of the general principle that, absent contrary direction, state officials and those with whom they deal are entitled to rely on a presumptively valid state statute, enacted in good faith and by no means plainly unlawful."

Hunt v. McNair, 413 U.S. 734 (1973)

Facts: A South Carolina statute authorized a financing arrangement between the State Educational Facilities Authority (Authority) and a Baptist college whereby the college would convey a substantial portion of its campus to the Authority, and the Authority would lease the property back to the college for exclusively secular use at an agreed rental. The Authority would then issue state revenue bonds in the amount of $3.5 million, which would be payable, principal and interest, from the rents paid by the college to the Authority under the lease. The proceeds of the sale of the bonds would be used to pay off outstanding indebtedness of the college and to construct additional buildings for use exclusively in connection with its secular higher education operations. Upon full payment of the bonds, the Authority was to reconvey title to the campus properties to the college. However, the Authority was empowered to revise the rent from time to time and otherwise scrutinize the operations and charges of the college. (The purpose of the financing arrangement was to enable the college to in effect borrow money at a significantly lower rate of interest than it would be forced to pay if it borrowed the money by conventional financing because the interest on the revenue bonds issued by the Authority was subject to neither federal nor state income taxes.) This proposed financing arrangement was unsuccessfully challenged as unconstitutional in violation of the Establishment Clause in the South Carolina Supreme Court.

Question: Does the proposed financing arrangement between the Authority and the Baptist college violate the Establishment Clause?

Decision: No. Opinion by Justice Powell. Vote: 6-3.

Reasons: To satisfy the Establishment Clause, a statute must have a secular legislative purpose, must have a principal or primary effect that neither advances nor inhibits religion, and must not foster an excessive governmental entanglement with religion. The purpose of the challenged financing arrangement is clearly secular: to further the opportunities of youth to attend quality higher educational institutions. The financing arrangement does not have a primary effect of advancing religion. The college places no religious qualifications for faculty membership or student admission, and only 60 percent of the student body is Baptist. Moreover, any assistance from the Authority relates only to land or buildings used exclusively for secular purposes. Lastly, the Court concluded that the proposed financing arrangement did not involve an unconstitutional entanglement between church and state. Any policing the Authority would conduct over facilities to ensure their secular use would not be excessive, especially since religious indoctrination is not a substantial purpose of the college. Any day-to-day supervision by the Authority over the college would occur only if the college defaulted on its bonds, a situation not presently before the Court. Under the three-pronged test governing Establishment Clause questions, the Court thus held that the proposed financing arrangement between the Authority and the college was constitutional.

U.S. Civil Service Commission v. Letter Carriers, 413 U.S. 548 (1973)

Facts: Section 9(a) of the Hatch Act, prohibiting federal employees from taking "an active part in political management or in political campaigns" was successfully attacked as unconstitutional on its face in lower federal court on the grounds of vagueness and overbreadth. The phrase in section 9(a) that was challenged defined political activity as "those acts of political campaigning which were prohibited on the part of employees in the competitive service before July 19, 1940, by determinations of the Civil Service Commission. . . ."

Question: Is section 9(a) of the Hatch Act unconstitutionally vague or overbroad?

Decision: No. Opinion by Justice White. Vote: 6-3.

Reasons: The Court first reaffirmed its holding in *United Public Workers* v. *Mitchell,* 330 U.S. 75 (1947), that neither the First Amendment nor any other constitutional provision bars a statute forbidding partisan political conduct by federal employees.

Turning to the questions of vagueness and overbreadth the Court stated that these issues should be tested against Civil Service Commission regulations restating the law of forbidden political activity under section 9(a) and the express words of that section. The Court found nothing vague in the words "taking active part in political management or in political campaigns," especially since the Hatch Act specifically provides that the employee retains the right to vote as he chooses and to express his opinion on political subjects and candidates. Regarding the commission regulations specifying particular conduct that would be prohibited or permitted, the Court did not find them impermissibly vague.

There might be quibbles about the meaning of taking an "active part in managing" or about "actively participating in fund raising" or about the meaning of becoming a "partisan" candidate for office; but there are limitations in the English language with respect to being both specific and manageably brief, and it seems to us that although the prohibitions may not satisfy those intent on finding fault at any cost, they are set out in terms that the ordinary person exercising ordinary common sense can sufficiently understand and comply with, without sacrifice to the public interest.

The Court added that it was also important that the commission would give advice as to the legality of any proposed course of action under section 9(a).

The Court also concluded that the challenged commission regulations forbade only activity likely to occur in partisan political campaigning and thus were not overbroad.

Broadrick v. Oklahoma, 413 U.S. 601 (1973)

Facts: Oklahoma state employees, charged by the Oklahoma State Personnel Board with actively engaging in partisan political activities (including the solicitation of money) among their coworkers for the benefit of their superior, in violation of section 818 of the state merit system act, challenged the constitutionality of that section on the grounds that two of its paragraphs were vague and overbroad in restricting constitutionally protected political activity. One paragraph provided that "[n]o employee in the classified service . . . shall, directly or indirectly, solicit, receive, or in any manner be concerned in soliciting or receiving any assessment . . . or contribution for any political organization, candidacy or other political purpose." The other provided that no such employee shall belong to "any national, state or local committee of a political party" or be an officer or member of a committee or a partisan political club, or a candidate for any paid public office, or take part in the management or affairs of any political party or campaign "except to exercise his right as a citizen privately to express his opinion and . . . vote." (Violation of section 818 results in dismissal from employment and possible criminal sanctions and limited eligibility for state employment.)

Question: Are the challenged paragraphs of section 818 unconstitutionally vague or overbroad?

Decision: No. Opinion by Justice White. Vote: 5-4.

Reasons: Section 818 is not so vague that "men of common intelligence must necessarily guess at its meaning." The challenged paragraphs proscribe certain political activity in plain language. "Words inevitably contain germs of uncertainty . . . [but] 'there are limitations in the English language with respect to being both specific and manageably brief' " and the challenged paragraphs are sufficiently specific to enable persons to comply therewith without deterring constitutionally protected activity.

Regarding the contention that section 818 was overbroad, the Court noted that the partisan political conduct for which the state employees were charged was clearly constitutionally unprotected. The Court concluded that, even if section 818 might conceivably be applied in an unconstitutional manner to other persons in other situations not before the Court, these state employees had no standing to raise that issue because the section was not "substantially" overbroad. Before persons charged with engaging in constitutionally unprotected conduct can challenge a statute restricting First Amendment freedoms of speech and association on the ground of overbreadth, the "overbreadth . . . must not only be real, but substantial as well, judged in relation to the statute's plainly legitimate sweep."

Pittsburgh Press Co. v. Pittsburgh Human Relations Commission, 413 U.S. 376 (1973)

Facts: A Pittsburgh Human Relations Ordinance (Ordinance) prohibited newspapers from carrying "help-wanted" advertisements in sex-designated columns except where the employer or advertiser could lawfully prefer one sex in hiring or employment referral decisions. The Ordinance was challenged as unconstitutional in violation of the freedoms of speech and press guaranteed by the First Amendment.

Question: Does the challenged Ordinance violate the First Amendment?

Decision: No. Opinion by Justice Powell. Vote: 5-4.

Reasons: Valentine v. *Chrestensen,* 316 U.S. 52 (1942), established the doctrine that commercial speech is not constitutionally immune from governmental regulation under the First Amendment. The challenged Ordinance in this case does affect the make-up of the help-wanted section of the newspaper; but the advertisements themselves, expressing no opinions on matters of social policy, are classic examples of commercial speech and thus may be constitutionally regulated. Moreover, the lower court found that placing want ads in sex-designated columns aided employers in illegally practicing sex discrimination.

> Any First Amendment interest which might be served by advertising an ordinary commercial proposal and which might arguably outweigh the governmental interest supporting the regulation is altogether absent when the commercial activity is itself illegal and the restriction on advertising is incidental to a valid limitation on economic activity.

The Court also rejected a contention that the Ordinance imposed an unconstitutional prior restraint on speech by permitting the Human Relations Commission to issue a cease-and-desist order forbidding the use of sex-designated help-wanted columns. Reasoning that the special vice of prior restraint is that communication will be suppressed before an adequate determination can be made that it is unprotected by the First Amendment, the Court concluded that the vice was not present in this case because the cease-and-desist order did not endanger arguably protected speech.

41

Columbia Broadcasting System, Inc. v. Democratic National Committee, 412
U.S. 94 (1973)

Facts: The Business Executives' Move for Vietnam Peace (BEM), a national
organization of businessmen opposed to United States involvement in the Vietnam
conflict, filed a complaint with the Federal Communications Commission (FCC)
against radio station WTOP for refusing to sell BEM time to broadcast a series of
one-minute spot announcements expressing their views. A WTOP policy forbade
the selling of time for spot announcements to individuals and groups wishing to
expound their views on controversial issues. BEM contended WTOP's policy
violated the First Amendment and the Federal Communications Act (Act). A
short while later, the Democratic National Committee (DNC) sought a declaratory ruling from the FCC that a broadcaster could not, consistent with the First
Amendment and the Act, refuse to sell time, as a general policy, to responsible
entities for comment on public issues. The FCC rejected both the BEM and DNC
claims, ruling that neither the First Amendment nor the Act prohibited broadcasters from maintaining a flat ban on paid public issue announcements, even
though other sorts of paid announcements were accepted.

Question: Does the First Amendment or the Act prohibit broadcasters from
refusing, as a general policy, to sell time for comment on public issues?

Decision: No. Opinion by Chief Justice Burger. Vote: 7-2.

Reasons: The whole history of the Act makes clear "that Congress intended
to permit private broadcasting to develop with the widest journalistic freedom
consistent with its public obligations." Because the First Amendment restricts only
"governmental action," the extent of governmental regulation of broadcast licensees must be scrutinized to determine whether in this case the decision to refuse to sell time to the DNC and BEM can properly be deemed governmental
action.

The regulatory scheme over broadcaster licensees established in the Act
makes the FCC a general overseer but places primary responsibility for fairness,
balance and objectivity on the licensee. In this case, the FCC has not fostered
the challenged licensee policy but has simply declined to take action with regard
to WTOP's policy because it fell within the area of journalistic discretion. The
Court thus concluded that the broadcasters' policy of refusing to sell time for
comment on public issues was not governmental action because the government
was not a "partner" to the decision and did not profit from the challenged policy.
A contrary conclusion, the Court noted, "would go far in practical effect to undermine nearly a half century of unmistakable congressional purpose to maintain—
no matter how difficult the task—essentially private broadcast journalism held
only broadly accountable to public interest standards."

The Court also rejected the contention that the Act's requirement that broadcasters operate in the "public interest" mandated that broadcasters accept editorial advertisements. Congress has several times indicated that whether individuals should have private rights of access to broadcast time should be left to

the FCC. The FCC was justified in concluding that the public interest in providing access to the marketplace of ideas and experiences would not be served if a private right of access was mandated because the affluent might thereby monopolize editorial advertising. "In the delicate balancing historically followed in the regulation of broadcasting, Congress and the Commission could appropriately conclude that the allocation of journalistic priorities should be concentrated in the licensee rather than diffused among many." Moreover, under a governmentally supervised right-of-access system, the FCC would be required to oversee the day-to-day operations of broadcasters, deciding such questions as whether a particular individual or group has had sufficient opportunity to present its viewpoint and whether a particular viewpoint has already been sufficiently aired; such close supervision would be contrary to the congressional purpose of maximizing the freedom of broadcasters over their journalistic decisions.

Criminal Law and Procedure

The Court decided 42 criminal cases this term and most of the decisions sustained the position of the prosecution on the issue involved, thereby indicating a trend in favor of stricter law enforcement. There were no dramatic decisions comparable to the ruling striking down the imposition of the death penalty last term in *Furman* v. *Georgia,* 408 U.S. 238 (1972). Since *Furman* was decided, several legislatures have passed new death penalty statutes that restrict the discretion to impose capital punishment in an attempt to satisfy constitutional requirements. *Furman* left open the question of whether evenhanded imposition of capital punishment would be constitutional.

The Court did not substantially expand the right to counsel this term as it has in past terms. The Court rejected the claim that an accused has a right to counsel whenever the government conducts a post-indictment interview with a witness to get an identification of the offender based upon photographs. In proceedings to revoke probation or parole, the Court held that whether counsel should be provided must be determined on a case-by-case basis.

Regarding obscenity laws, the Court made clear that only exigent circumstances would justify the warrantless seizure of allegedly obscene material. However, the Court ruled that an adversary hearing before a judicial officer was not constitutionally mandated before obscene materials could be seized pursuant to a warrant, at least when the seizure was to preserve the material as evidence and copies of the material were available for distribution to the public prior to any final determination of obscenity.

In several cases the Court expanded the rights of prisoners to seek habeas corpus relief. In one case, however, the justices rejected an attempt by prisoners to avoid the requirement that state remedies be exhausted before seeking habeas corpus in federal courts by characterizing their complaint as falling under federal civil rights laws.

The Court upheld government contentions that grand juries may compel witnesses to give voice and handwriting exemplars without any preliminary showing of reasonableness, that a warrantless taking of fingernail scrapings from a defendant over his objection was constitutional, that persons could validly consent to a search without knowledge of their right to refuse, that guilty pleas foreclosed any collateral attack based on constitutional infirmities in the government's case, that the defense of entrapment was unavailable to those "predisposed" to commit crime, and that the Fifth Amendment privilege against self-incrimination was not violated when a taxpayer's records were subpoenaed from her accountant.

The Court ruled in favor of the defense in holding that warrantless searches of cars anywhere within 100 miles of the border was unconstitutional and in striking down an Oregon law giving the state power to discover the accused's defenses before trial but not allowing the accused reciprocal discovery rights.

United States v. Ash, 413 U.S. 300 (1973)

Facts: A defendant sought to exclude certain evidence based on a post-indictment photographic identification made when defendant's counsel was not present. He argued that the identification was made in violation of his Sixth Amendment right to counsel.

Question: Does the Sixth Amendment grant an accused the right to have counsel present whenever the government conducts a post-indictment photographic display containing a picture of the accused for the purpose of allowing a witness to attempt an identification of the offender?

Decision: No. Opinion by Justice Blackmun. Vote: 6-3.

Reasons: The Sixth Amendment right to counsel attaches whenever the accused requires aid in coping with legal problems of such magnitude that the failure to provide counsel would be tantamount to depriving the accused of a fair trial. The presence of counsel at pre-trial interviews with witnesses when photographic identifications are made is unnecessary to preserve an accused's right to a fair trial. Defense counsel can effectively cross-examine any witness making photo identifications by reconstructing the photo display or by interviewing that witness before trial. The Court noted that the primary safeguard against improper tactics in prosecuting a case is the "ethical responsibility of the prosecutor . . .," and concluded that the risk of improper use of photographic displays was not so great as to require the presence of defense counsel.

Couch v. United States, 409 U.S. 322 (1973)

Facts: After the government subpoenaed her tax records from her accountant in connection with an investigation into her tax liability from 1964 to 1968, Couch sued to enjoin the government from compelling her accountant to produce those records in his possession on the ground that such compulsion violated her Fifth Amendment privilege against self-incrimination.

Question: Does compelling the production of incriminating documents owned by the taxpayer but in the possession of her accountant violate her Fifth Amendment privilege against compulsory self-incrimination?

Decision: No. Opinion by Justice Powell. Vote: 7-2.

Reasons: "[T]he Fifth Amendment privilege is a *personal* privilege: it adheres basically to the person, not to information which may incriminate him." In this case, since the subpoena was directed against the accountant, "the ingredient of personal compulsion against an accused is lacking." Although Couch owned the challenged documents, the Court stated that in general the Fifth Amendment privilege applied only to documents actually possessed and not merely owned. While agreeing that there might be circumstances where a person might either put documents in custody or lose their possession for such a short time that the Fifth Amendment privilege would remain, the Court concluded such circumstances were lacking in this case in which the challenged documents had been given regularly to the accountant since 1955, and the accountant neither worked in Couch's office nor as her employee. The Court also noted that no confidential accountant-client privilege exists under federal law.

United States v. Dionisio, 410 U.S. 1 (1973).

Facts: After a federal grand jury obtained certain voice recordings from court-authorized wiretaps issued in connection with the investigation of federal gambling laws, it subpoenaed approximately 20 persons, including Dionisio, seeking to obtain from them voice exemplars for comparison with the recorded conversations. After being advised that he was a potential defendant in a criminal prosecution and of his right to an attorney, Dionisio refused to give the grand jury a voice exemplar on the grounds that compelling him to provide voice exemplars violated his Fifth Amendment privilege against self-incrimination and his Fourth Amendment right against unreasonable searches and seizures. The government's petition to a lower federal court to compel Dionisio to furnish voice exemplars was ultimately denied on the grounds that "under the Fourth Amendment law enforcement officials may not compel the production of physical evidence absent a showing of the reasonableness of the seizure." The lower federal court thought that to permit the grand jury to compel voice exemplars without a prior showing of their reasonable relation to crime would subvert the Fourth Amendment's requirement that persons be arrested, searched, or seized only upon probable cause to believe they are implicated in crime.

Question: Does a witness's Fifth Amendment privilege against self-incrimination or Fourth Amendment right against unreasonable search and seizure prevent a grand jury from compelling him to furnish voice exemplars?

Decision: No. Opinion by Justice Stewart. Vote: 6-2.

Reasons: "It has long been held that the compelled display of identifiable physical characteristics infringes no interest protected by the privilege against compulsory self-incrimination," which applies only to testimonial or communicative evidence. In *Schmerber* v. *California,* 384 U.S. 757 (1964), the Court held that the extraction and chemical analysis of a blood sample violated no Fifth Amendment rights. In *Gilbert* v. *California,* 388 U.S. 263 (1967), and *United*

States v. *Wade,* 388 U.S. 218 (1967), the Court held that compelling defendants to furnish handwriting exemplars or to utter words allegedly spoken by a robber in a line-up was constitutionally permissible. Since the voice exemplars in the case were to be used solely to measure the physical properties of the witness's voice and not for their testimonial or communicative content, the Court concluded that compelling their production did not violate the Fifth Amendment.

The Court rejected Dionisio's Fourth Amendment claim on the ground that he had no reasonable expectation of keeping the physical characteristics of his voice private from a grand jury. In *Katz* v. *United States,* 389 U.S. 347 (1969), the Court held that under the Fourth Amendment, "whenever an individual may harbor a reasonable 'expectation of privacy,' . . . he is entitled to be free from unreasonable governmental intrusion." Reasoning that a subpoena to appear before a grand jury was not a seizure under the Fourth Amendment, that persons are obligated to appear and give evidence before a grand jury, and that receiving a subpoena involves no stigma or personal inconvenience since the time for appearance can be altered, the Court concluded that grand jury subpoenas were not an unreasonable governmental intrusion upon an individual, absent a showing of official harassment. The Court thus held that the grand jury could constitutionally compel Dionisio to furnish voice exemplars without any preliminary showing of the reasonableness of the request.

United States v. Mara, 410 U.S. 19 (1973)

Facts: After being informed that he was a potential criminal defendant in the matter under investigation, Mara resisted a federal grand jury subpoena to furnish handwriting and printing exemplars on the ground that such compulsion violated his Fourth Amendment right against unreasonable searches and seizures, unless the government made a preliminary showing of reasonableness. A lower federal court ruled that before the grand jury subpoena could be enforced, the government would have to show "that the grand jury was properly authorized . . ., that the information sought is relevant to the inquiry, . . . that . . . the grand jury process is not being abused . . ." and that satisfactory handwriting and printing exemplars cannot be obtained from other sources.

Question: Must the government make any preliminary showing of reasonableness before a grand jury can constitutionally compel handwriting and printing exemplars?

Decision: No. Opinion by Justice Stewart. Vote: 5-3.

Reasons: In *United States* v. *Dionisio,* 410 U.S. 1 (1973), the Court held that "a grand jury subpoena is not a 'seizure' within the meaning of the Fourth Amendment, and further, that the Amendment is not violated by a grand jury directive compelling production of physical characteristics which are constantly exposed to the public. Handwriting, like speech, is repeatedly shown to the public, and there is no more expectation of privacy in the physical characteristics of a person's script than there is in the tone of his voice. Consequently the Government was under no obligation here, any more than in *Dionisio,* to make a preliminary showing of reasonableness."

Cupp v. Murphy, 412 U.S. 291 (1973)

Facts: With probable cause to believe the defendant had murdered his wife by strangulation, the police, after the defendant had voluntarily come to the station house, noticed a dark spot on his finger which they suspected was dried blood. Without arresting the defendant, without a warrant, and over the defendant's protest, the police took a sample of his fingernail scrapings which turned out to contain traces of skin and blood cells, and fabric from the victim's nightgown. This evidence was introduced at the defendant's trial over the claim that it was the product of an unlawful search under the Fourth Amendment and thus not admissible.

Question: Did the police, in taking a sample of the defendant's fingernail scrapings without a warrant, violate his Fourth Amendment right against unreasonable searches?

Decision: No. Opinion by Justice Stewart. Vote: 7-2.

Reasons: The police search was constitutionally valid under the principles set forth in *Chimel* v. *California,* 395 U.S. 752 (1969), that recognize the right to make warrantless searches if incident to a valid arrest. Under *Chimel,* an arrestee may be searched without a warrant at the time of his arrest primarily because the arrestee may attempt to destroy incriminating evidence in his possession. In this case, the defendant had not been arrested, so that a full *Chimel* search without a warrant might not have been justified. However, the defendant gave signs of attempting to destroy the evidence under his fingernails and the very limited search was necessary to preserve this evidence. "On the facts of this case, considering the existence of probable cause, the very limited intrusion undertaken incident to the station house detention, and the ready destructibility of the evidence, we cannot say that this search violated the Fourth Amendment."

Cady v. Dombrowski, 413 U.S. 433 (1973)

Facts: After arresting a Chicago police officer for drunken driving, a Wisconsin policeman called a tow truck to remove the disabled car to a privately owned service station and conducted a warrantless search looking for a revolver which Chicago policemen were required to carry at all times. Unexpectedly, the search uncovered evidence of blood which ultimately led to murder charges against the Chicago policeman. At trial, the defendant policeman sought to suppress any evidence uncovered by the warrantless search of his car or the fruits thereof on the ground that the search was unreasonable and thus in violation of his Fourth Amendment rights.

Question: Did the challenged warrantless search violate the defendant's Fourth Amendment rights against unreasonable searches and seizures?

Decision: No. Opinion by Justice Rehnquist. Vote: 5-4.

Reasons: The ultimate standard set forth in the Fourth Amendment to determine the constitutionality of searches is reasonableness. In this case, the search of the car to look for a revolver to prevent it from falling into improper hands was standard procedure. The car was towed to a private garage for elementary reasons of safety. Moreover, the search was not conducted with any intent to uncover evidence of the murder for which the defendant was ultimately tried. Although recognizing the general rule that warrantless searches are unreasonable except when made in special circumstances, the Court concluded that the challenged search of the car, which the police reasonably believed contained a gun, was reasonable within the meaning of the Fourth Amendment.

Almeida-Sanchez v. United States, 413 U.S. 266 (1973)

Facts: Section 287(a) of the Immigration and Nationality Act provides for warrantless searches of automobiles and other conveyances "within a reasonable distance from any external boundary of the United States" as authorized by regulations to be promulgated by the attorney general. The attorney general's regulation defines "reasonable distance" as within 100 air miles from any external boundary of the United States. Pursuant to section 287(a) and the attorney general's regulation, the United States Border Patrol stopped and conducted a warrantless search of a Mexican citizen's car about 25 miles north of the California-Mexico border, without probable cause to believe the car contained aliens or had made a border crossing. The search uncovered marijuana, evidence which the Mexican sought to suppress in a subsequent criminal proceeding on the ground that the search leading to its discovery violated the Fourth Amendment.

Question: Did the warrantless search of the car conducted without probable cause to suspect or without even reasonable suspicion of unlawful activity violate the Fourth Amendment?

Decision: Yes. Opinion by Justice Stewart. Vote: 5-4.

Reasons: Prior case law concerning warrantless searches of automobiles when probable cause does exist and warrantless administrative inspections justified by the practicalities of supervising intensively regulated industries provide no support for the challenged search in this case made without either a warrant or probable cause. Further, the statute and regulation authorizing the search together violate the Fourth Amendment's prohibition against unreasonable searches and seizures because they give law enforcement authorities unfettered discretion to stop and search anyone within 100 miles of a border. While noting the right of the government to conduct routine inspections and searches of individuals or conveyances seeking to cross our borders, the Court concluded that the searches authorized by the statute and regulation went far beyond border searches or the functional equivalent of the same.

Roaden v. Kentucky, 413 U.S. 496 (1973)

Facts: After viewing a sexually explicit film, a sheriff arrested the theatre manager for exhibiting an obscene film in violation of Kentucky law and without obtaining a warrant seized one copy of the film for use as evidence. At trial on the obscenity charge, the manager sought to suppress evidence of the film on the ground that it was seized in violation of the Fourth Amendment.

Question: Was the warrantless seizure of the allegedly obscene film unconstitutional under the Fourth Amendment?

Decision: Yes. Opinion by Chief Justice Burger. Vote: 5-4.

Reasons: The Fourth Amendment prohibits "unreasonable" seizures. Whether seizures are constitutionally unreasonable must be determined from the totality of circumstances. The warrantless seizure of the film in this case was unreasonable, not simply because the securing of a warrant would have been easy, "but rather because prior restraint of the right of expression, whether by books or films, calls for a higher hurdle in the evaluation of reasonableness." Moreover, there were no exigent circumstances in this case requiring the sheriff to seize the film without a warrant in order to avoid losing evidence of the crime.

Heller v. New York, 413 U.S. 483 (1973)

Facts: Upon viewing a film depicting a nude couple engaged in ultimate sexual acts, a judge signed a warrant for its seizure because he deemed the film obscene under New York statutes. The warrant was immediately executed by police officers and the theatre manager was arrested and charged with violating New York obscenity laws. No motion was made before trial for the return of the film or for its suppression as evidence. Nor did the defendant claim that seizure of the film prevented its exhibition by use of another copy. During trial, the defendant unsuccessfully contended that seizure of the film without a prior adversary hearing violated the Fourteenth Amendment and required dismissal of the charges against him.

Question: Can a judicial officer, after viewing a film and finding it to be obscene, constitutionally issue a warrant for its seizure without first conducting an adversary hearing on the issue of probable obscenity?

Decision: Yes. Opinion by Chief Justice Burger. Vote: 5-4.

Reasons: Prior case law has neither held nor implied that there is an absolute First or Fourteenth Amendment right to a prior adversary hearing applicable to all cases where allegedly obscene material is seized. A judicial determination of obscenity in an adversary proceeding is required before imposing a final restraint on the suppressed material, but not before an initial seizure of the alleged obscene material for temporary detention to preserve it as evidence. The seized film in this case was not subjected to any final restraint before or during trial because a copy was always available for showing. The Court concluded that seizure of a film pursuant to a valid warrant issued upon probable cause of its obscenity, if followed by a prompt judicial determination of the obscenity issue in an adversary proceeding during which time a copy of the film is available for showing, is constitutionally permissible.

Schneckloth v. Bustamonte, 412 U.S. 218 (1973)

Facts: Police searched the defendant's car, without a warrant and without probable cause to arrest him, after the defendant's brother had verbally consented to the search. The search turned up evidence that was used at the defendant's trial to convict him. Finding that in all the circumstances of this case the consent to search was given to the policy voluntarily, the trial judge denied the defendant's motion to suppress the evidence on the ground that the consent could not be constitutionally valid unless given by a person with actual knowledge of his legal right to withhold his consent. (In the circumstances of this case, the challenged search would have been unconstitutional under the Fourth Amendment unless consent was validly given.)

Question: To prove that a person has voluntarily consented to a search, thereby waiving his right under the Fourth Amendment to otherwise prevent the search without a warrant, must the state prove that such person had actual knowledge of his constitutional right to withhold his consent?

Decision: No. Opinion by Justice Stewart. Vote: 6-3.

Reasons: Prior case law concerning voluntary confessions indicates that the constitutional definition of "voluntariness" has reflected an accommodation of the complex values implicated in the policeman's need to gather evidence for effective law enforcement and the citizen's need for protection from possible police overreaching. The determination of voluntariness of confessions in these cases turned on an evaluation of all the circumstances, including whether the accused knew he had a right to refuse to answer the questions put to him. The need to accommodate the police need for evidence to enforce the criminal laws effectively while protecting citizens against unconstitutional searches compels the conclusion that "the question whether a consent to search was in fact 'voluntary' or was the product of duress or coercion, express or implied, is a question of fact to be determined from the totality of circumstances. . . . [W]hile the subject's knowledge of a right to refuse is a factor to be taken into account, the prosecution is not required to demonstrate such knowledge as prerequisite to establishing a voluntary consent."

The Court distinguished other cases requiring actual knowledge of a defendant's constitutional rights before waiver of those rights would be deemed valid, for example, *Johnson* v. *Zerbst,* 304 U.S. 458 (1938) (waiver of right to counsel), and *Miranda* v. *Arizona,* 384 U.S. 436 (1966) (waiver of right against self-incrimination), on the ground that the rights waived in those cases were essential to preserving a defendant's right to a fair trial. The protections of the Fourth Amendment, the Court reasoned, "have nothing whatever to do with promoting the fair ascertainment of truth at a criminal trial" but guarantee the security of one's privacy against arbitrary police intrusion. The Court concluded that because invalid searches were less harmful than convictions of innocent persons, the standards of waiver pertaining to searches could rationally be less stringent than those standards pertaining to waiver of constitutional rights affecting the integrity of the truth-finding process at trial.

Brown v. United States, 411 U.S. 223 (1973)

Facts: Two defendants convicted of transporting stolen goods and of conspiracy to transport stolen goods in violation of 18 U.S. Code, 2314 and 18 U.S. Code, 371 challenged their convictions on the ground that evidence introduced against them was unconstitutionally seized from a coconspirator (who was tried separately). Although they had no proprietary or possessory interest in the coconspirator's premises from which the challenged evidence (stolen merchandise) was illegally seized, the defendants contended that they nevertheless had standing to object to the admissibility of such evidence because (1) they were coconspirators with a person who had had his constitutional rights invaded, and (2) under *Jones* v. *United States,* 362 U.S. 257 (1962), anyone has standing to contest the admissibility of evidence stemming from an illegal search where the possession needed to establish standing is also an essential element of the offense charged.

Question: Did the defendants have standing to challenge the admissibility into evidence of stolen goods that were illegally seized from a coconspirator either because of their relation to the coconspirator or because of the automatic standing rule announced in *Jones* v. *United States?*

Decision: No. Opinion by Chief Justice Burger. Vote: 9-0.

Reasons: Jones v. *United States* is inapplicable to this case because the government's case against the defendants did not depend on their possession of the challenged evidence at the time of the illegal search. The stolen goods seized in the search had been transported and sold by the defendants to their coconspirator two months before such search, and the conspiracy and transportation charges alleged by the indictment against the defendants were limited to the period before the day of the search.

The Court rejected the argument that the defendants had standing to challenge an illegal search directed against their coconspirator, relying on its past decisions clearly holding that "Fourth Amendment rights are personal rights which, like some other constitutional rights, may not be vicariously asserted."

United States v. Russell, 411 U.S. 423 (1973)

Facts: After a jury trial in federal district court in which his sole defense was entrapment, Russell was convicted of having unlawfully manufactured and processed methamphetamine ("speed") and having unlawfully sold and delivered that drug in violation of federal law. The court of appeals reversed the conviction solely for the reason that an undercover agent supplied an essential chemical for manufacturing the "speed" which formed the basis of Russell's conviction and held that "a defense to a criminal charge may be founded upon an intolerable degree of governmental participation in the criminal enterprise."

Question: Did the court of appeals err in holding that an entrapment defense may be founded solely upon an intolerable degree of governmental participation in the criminal enterprise for which the defendant is being prosecuted?

Decision: Yes. Opinion by Justice Rehnquist. Vote: 5-4.

Reasons: In *Sorrells* v. *United States,* 287 U.S. 435 (1932), and *Sherman* v. *United States,* 356 U.S. 369 (1958), the Court concluded that entrapment as a defense to a criminal prosecution may be established only if the government's activity actually implants the criminal design in the defendant's mind but that such defense is not established if the defendant had a "predisposition" to commit the charged offenses. The Court refused to broaden the definition of entrapment as set forth in *Sorrells* and *Sherman* and thus held that the court of appeals erred in concluding that an intolerable degree of governmental participation in a crime, even when the defendant harbored a predisposition to commit the crime, could establish an entrapment defense. In this case, a government agent supplied the defendant with a chemical element necessary for the defendant's manufacture of "speed." However, since the defendant was predisposed to commit the narcotics offenses for which he was charged, he could not avail himself of the entrapment defense. The Court reserved the question of whether in some other case the conduct of law enforcement agents might be so outrageous as to absolutely bar the government under due process principles from invoking judicial processes to obtain a conviction.

Wardius v. Oregon, 412 U.S. 470 (1973)

Facts: An Oregon statute required defendants in criminal actions proposing to rely upon an alibi defense to notify the prosecuting attorney five days in advance of trial of all evidence he intended to use to establish the alibi. However, the statute did not require the prosecuting attorney to give the defendant "reciprocal discovery" through notice to the defendant in advance of trial of evidence the state proposed to use to discredit any alibi defense. The Oregon statute was challenged as unconstitutional on the ground that the lack of reciprocal discovery concerning alibi defenses was so unfair as to violate due process.

Question: Does the Due Process Clause of the Fourteenth Amendment forbid enforcement of state alibi rules unless reciprocal discovery rights are given to criminal defendants?

Decision: Yes. Opinion by Justice Marshall. Vote: 9-0.

Reasons: "Notice of alibi rules . . . are based on the proposition that the ends of justice will best be served by a system of liberal discovery which gives both parties the maximum possible amount of information with which to prepare their cases and thereby reduces the possibility of surprise at trial." However, the challenged Oregon statute, while requiring defendants to give pre-trial notice of any alibi defense, grants no discovery rights to criminal defendants.

[I]n the absence of a strong showing of state interests to the contrary, discovery must be a two-way street. The State may not insist that trials be run as a search for truth so far as defense witnesses are concerned, while maintaining poker game secrecy for its own witnesses. It is fundamentally unfair to require a defendant to divulge the details of his own case while at the same time subjecting him to the hazard of surprise concerning refutation of the very pieces of evidence which he disclosed to the State.

Because the state failed to prove any governmental interests justifying lack of reciprocity in its challenged discovery statute, the Court declared that statute unconstitutional in violation of due process.

Ward v. *Village of Monroeville, Ohio*, 409 U.S. 57 (1972)

Facts: The mayor of Monroeville, having wide executive powers and being the president of the village council and the chief conservator of the peace, also sits as a judge in cases of ordinance violations and certain traffic offenses pursuant to an Ohio statute. A truck driver, having been convicted by the mayor of two traffic offenses and fined $100, appealed his conviction, contending he was denied his due process right to be tried by an impartial judicial officer, although he was entitled to a trial *de novo* in the county court of common pleas.

Question: Do criminal trials before a mayor having responsibilities for revenue production, law enforcement, and other executive tasks deny defendants their due process rights to be tried before a disinterested and impartial judicial officer, even though defendants are entitled to a trial *de novo* in another court?

Decision: Yes. Opinion by Justice Brennan. Vote: 7-2.

Reasons: In *Tumey* v. *Ohio,* 273 U.S. 510 (1927), the Court held that fines levied by a mayor whose salary was partly paid from those fines were invalid under the Due Process Clause of the Fourteenth Amendment. In that case, the Court held that a judge does not possess the requisite impartiality demanded by due process if he occupies a position "which would offer a possible temptation to the average man as a judge to forget the burden of proof required to convict the defendant or which might lead him not to hold the balance nice, clear, and true between the State and the accused. . . ." The Court concluded that in this case, where 25-50 percent of total village revenues were raised from the fines, forfeitures, costs and fees imposed by the mayor's court, the mayor of Monroeville occupied "two practically and seriously inconsistent positions, one partisan and the other judicial," so that the trials of defendants charged with crime before him were inconsistent with due process of law. Viewing the right to a trial *de novo* before an impartial judge to be constitutionally irrelevant, the Court held that defendants are "entitled to a neutral and detached judge in the first instance." The Court specifically left open the question of whether it would be unconstitutional to permit a mayor or similar official to serve in essentially a ministerial capacity in a traffic or ordinance violation case in order to accept a free and voluntary plea of guilty or *nolo contendere,* a forfeiture of collateral, or the like.

Chambers v. Mississippi, 410 U.S. 284 (1973)

Facts: Chambers, convicted in a Mississippi court of murdering a policeman and sentenced to life imprisonment, claimed he was denied a fair trial in violation of due process because the trial judge prevented him from introducing exculpatory evidence. Shortly after the murder, Gable McDonald, a lifelong resident of the area, made a written confession to Chambers's attorneys and on three separate occasions orally confessed the killing to three different friends. McDonald later repudiated these confessions and was never brought to trial. At his trial, Chambers called McDonald as a witness and introduced McDonald's written confession. When McDonald repudiated his confession during cross-examination by the state, Chambers moved to declare McDonald an adverse witness so that he could impeach McDonald's testimony by introducing evidence of McDonald's three oral confessions. (Under Mississippi law a party may impeach only adverse witnesses.) Chambers's motion was denied, and the testimony of the three witnesses to whom McDonald had confessed was excluded on the ground that their testimony as to McDonald's statements was hearsay.

Question: Did the Mississippi trial court's evidentiary rulings preventing Chambers from introducing exculpatory evidence deny him a fair trial in violation of due process?

Decision: Yes. Opinion by Justice Powell. Vote: 8-1.

Reasons: "The right of an accused in a criminal trial to due process is in essence the right of a fair opportunity to defend against the State's accusations." Chambers was denied the opportunity to subject McDonald's damning repudiation of his earlier confessions to cross-examination, even though the confessions clearly tended to exculpate Chambers. Chambers was thereby substantially denied his Sixth Amendment right to confront the witnesses against him. Moreover, Chambers was restricted in exercising his fundamental right to present witnesses in his own defense by the exclusion of the testimony of three witnesses stating that McDonald had confessed the murder to them. Although the testimony was technically hearsay, it was highly reliable because McDonald had no motives for fabrication. "We conclude that the exclusion of this critical evidence, coupled with the State's refusal to permit Chambers to cross-examine McDonald, denied him a trial in accord with tradition and fundamental standards of due process."

Barnes v. United States, 412 U.S. 837 (1973)

Facts: Charged with the knowing possession of United States Treasury checks stolen from the mails, the defendant objected to the district court's jury instruction that "[p]ossession of recently stolen property, if not satisfactorily explained, is ordinarily a circumstance from which you may reasonably draw the inference and find . . . that the person in possession knew the property had been stolen." The defendant contended that permitting a jury to infer knowledge that property was stolen from its unexplained possession was so arbitrary as to violate due process.

Question: Is the inference of guilty knowledge drawn from the fact of unexplained possession of stolen goods so arbitrary as to violate due process?

Decision: No. Decision by Justice Powell. Vote: 6-3.

Reasons: Prior case law teaches that a jury may constitutionally infer that a fact has been proven in a criminal case if the evidence necessary to invoke the inference is sufficient for a rational juror to find the inferred fact either beyond a reasonable doubt or by a preponderance of the evidence. In this case, the evidence established that the defendant possessed recently stolen treasury checks payable to persons he did not know, without plausible explanation for such possession consistent with innocence. "Such evidence was clearly sufficient to enable a jury to find beyond a reasonable doubt that . . . [the defendant] knew the checks were stolen." Since the inference of guilty knowledge from unexplained possession satisfied the reasonable doubt standard, the challenged jury instruction satisfied the requirements of due process.

The Court also rejected as insubstantial the contention that the challenged jury instruction violated the defendant's right against self-incrimination by emphasizing the failure to explain his possession of the stolen checks. "The mere massing of evidence against a defendant cannot be regarded as a violation of his privilege against self-incrimination."

Douglas v. Buder, 412 U.S. 430 (1973)

Facts: A Missouri probationer had his probation revoked after a hearing because he failed for 11 days to report an arrest (a traffic citation) in violation of the conditions of probation, although both the probation officer and the prosecutor took the position that the conditions of probation had not been violated and that probation should be continued. Under Missouri law, the issuance of a traffic citation is not an arrest.

Question: Was the finding that the Missouri probationer had violated the conditions of his probation by failing to report all arrests without delay so totally devoid of evidentiary support as to be invalid under the Due Process Clause of the Fourteenth Amendment?

Decision: Yes. Per curiam opinion. Vote: 8-0.

Reasons: At the time the probationer failed to report his traffic citation, nothing in Missouri law would have led him to believe that the issuance of that citation was an "arrest." Even if Missouri courts were to interpret a traffic citation to be the equivalent of an arrest, the application of that interpretation to the probationer's conditions of probation would not have been foreseeable in this case. Thus the finding violates due process because the probationer did not have fair warning that failure to report a traffic citation would cause the revocation of his probation. The Court determined that the revocation of the probationer's probation was so devoid of evidentiary or other legally supportable reasons as to violate due process.

Gagnon v. Scarpelli, 411 U.S. 778 (1973)

Facts: Scarpelli, having pled guilty to a charge of armed robbery and placed on probation for seven years in the custody of the Wisconsin Department of Public Welfare, had his probation revoked without a hearing and without being supplied with counsel. A lower federal court held that revocation of Scarpelli's probation without a hearing and without counsel deprived him of liberty without due process in violation of the Constitution.

Question: Does the Due Process Clause constitutionally entitle probationers to a hearing (in all cases) and to representation by counsel (in some cases) before his probation may be revoked?

Decision: Yes. Opinion by Justice Powell. Vote: 8-1.

Reasons: In *Morrissey* v. *Brewer*, 408 U.S. 471 (1972), the Court held that parole could not constitutionally be revoked unless the parolee is given a preliminary hearing to determine whether there is probable cause to believe that he has committed a violation of his parole followed by a comprehensive hearing prior to making a final decision on parole revocation. The Court reasoned that there is no difference between the revocation of parole and the revocation of probation as far as due process is concerned. Thus a probationer is entitled to preliminary and final revocation hearings under the conditions specified in *Morrissey* v. *Brewer*.

The Court then turned to the question of whether an indigent probationer or parolee has a due process right to be represented by appointed counsel at the revocation hearings. Reasoning that the purposes of the hearings were to afford the parolee or probationer an opportunity to establish that he had not violated any of the conditions on his freedom or, if he had violated those conditions, an opportunity to present mitigating facts justifying nonrevocation, the Court concluded that in some circumstances these purposes could be served only by providing the parolee or probationer with counsel. In specifically rejecting the contention that counsel must be afforded in all revocation hearings and in holding that whether counsel should be supplied should be determined on a case-by-case basis, the Court stated that "[p]resumptively . . . counsel should be provided in cases where, after being informed of his right to request counsel, the probationer or parolee makes such a request, based on a timely and colorful claim (i) that he has not committed the alleged violation of the conditions upon which he is at liberty; or (ii) that, even if the violation is a matter of public record or is uncontested, there are substantial reasons which justified or mitigated the violation and make revocation inappropriate and that the reasons are complex or otherwise difficult to develop or present." The Court added that the ability of the probationer or parolee to speak for himself should be considered in deciding whether counsel should be appointed and that, whenever a request for counsel was denied, the grounds for such refusal should be succinctly stated in the record.

Fontaine v. United States, 411 U.S. 213 (1973)

Facts: After he pleaded guilty to a bank robbery charge before a federal judge and was sentenced to 20 years' imprisonment, Fontaine moved to vacate his sentence under 28 U.S. Code, 2255 on the ground that his earlier plea of guilty had been induced by a combination of fear, coercive police tactics and mental illness. The federal district judge, before whom Fontaine had pleaded guilty and had acknowledged at the time that his plea was given knowingly and voluntarily, denied the motion to vacate without holding an evidentiary hearing reasoning that Fontaine could not collaterally attack the voluntariness of his plea.

Question: Was Fontaine entitled to an evidentiary hearing under 28 U.S. Code, 2255 to determine the voluntariness of his guilty plea?

Decision: Yes. Per curiam opinion. Vote: 8-1.

Reasons: "It is elementary that a coerced plea is open to collateral attack. . . . It is equally clear that section 2255 calls for a hearing on such allegations [of a coerced plea] unless 'the motion and the files and records of the case conclusively show that the prisoner is entitled to no relief. . . .' " In this case, Fontaine alleged he suffered physical abuse, mental and physical illness requiring hospitalization, and prolonged interrogation during the period preceding his plea. "On this record, we cannot conclude with the assurance required by the statutory standard 'conclusively show' that under no circumstances could . . . [Fontaine] establish facts warranting relief under Section 2255. . . ." Thus, Fontaine was entitled to a hearing on his petition in the district court.

Ham v. South Carolina, 409 U.S. 524 (1973)

Facts: During an examination of potential jurors on *voir dire* to determine any possible prejudice they might harbor against a bearded Negro defendant, the trial judge refused to ask questions requested by the defendant designed to elicit any racial prejudice or prejudice against beards. After he was convicted by a jury, the defendant challenged his conviction on the ground that the refusal of the trial judge to ask the requested questions denied him his constitutional right to a fair trial.

Question: Did the trial judge's refusal to ask the potential jurors requested questions designed to elicit racial prejudice or prejudice against beards deny the defendant his constitutional right to a fair trial?

Decision: Only the refusal to ask the question dealing with racial prejudice denied the defendant his constitutional rights. Opinion by Justice Rehnquist. Vote: 7-2.

Reasons: "Since one of the purposes of the Due Process Clause of the Fourteenth Amendment is to insure . . . [the] essential elements of fairness . . . and since a principal purpose of the adoption of the Fourteenth Amendment was to prohibit the States from invidiously discriminating on the basis of race . . . we think that the Fourteenth Amendment required the judge in this case to interrogate the jurors upon the subject of racial prejudice." Although agreeing that one or more of the potential jurors might have harbored prejudice against people with beards, the Court nevertheless concluded that "[given] the traditionally broad discretion accorded to the trial judge in conducting *voir dire* . . . and our inability to constitutionally distinguish possible prejudice against beards from a host of other possible similar prejudices, we do not believe the petitioner's constitutional rights were violated when the trial judge refused to put this question [about beards]."

Strunk v. United States, 412 U.S. 434 (1973)

Facts: After finding that the defendant had been deprived of his Sixth Amendment right to a speedy trial, a federal court of appeals held that the charges against the defendant should not be dismissed and remanded the case to the district court, where the defendant had earlier been convicted and sentenced, directing that court to reduce the sentence by 259 days "in order to compensate for the unnecessary delay which had occurred between return of the indictment and . . . [defendant's] arraignment." The defendant contended that once a judicial determination had been made that an accused had been unconstitutionally denied a speedy trial, the only remedy available to the court is to reverse the conviction, vacate the sentence and dismiss the indictment.

Question: Is the only constitutionally permissible remedy for a violation of the Sixth Amendment right to a speedy trial a dismissal of all charges against the defendant?

Decision: Yes. Opinion by Chief Justice Burger. Vote: 9-0.

Reasons: In *Barker* v. *Wingo,* 407 U.S. 514 (1972), the Court stated that among the purposes of the speedy trial guarantee was prevention of undue emotional stress on an accused facing the prospect of a public trial as well as prevention of any adverse effects on the prospects for rehabilitation when another sentence was being served. "In light of the policies which underlie the right to a speedy trial, dismissal must remain . . . 'the only possible remedy.' "

Braden v. 30th Judicial Circuit Court of Kentucky, 410 U.S. 484 (1973)

Facts: Braden, serving a 10-year sentence in an Alabama prison, applied to the U.S. District Court for Western Kentucky for a writ of habeas corpus under 28 U.S. Code, 2254 alleging a denial of his constitutional right to a speedy trial in Kentucky state court. He requested that an order issue directing Kentucky to afford him an immediate trial on a then three-year-old indictment. Kentucky had issued a detainer against Braden in Alabama directing that he be released into Kentucky's custody after the completion of his sentence in Alabama. Braden alleged that he had made repeated demands for a speedy trial on the Kentucky indictment, that he had been denied his right to a speedy trial, that further delay would impair his ability to defend himself, and that the existence of the Kentucky indictment prejudiced his opportunity for parole in Alabama. Over Kentucky's objection that the district court lacked jurisdiction over Braden's petition under 28 U.S. Code, 2241(a) which limits district courts to granting writs of habeas corpus "within their respective jurisdictions" and that Braden had not exhausted his state remedies as required by 28 U.S. Code, 2254, the U.S. District Court for Western Kentucky granted Braden's writ of federal habeas corpus.

Questions: Did the district court have jurisdiction to hear Braden's petition for habeas corpus under 28 U.S. Code, 2241(a)? Did Braden exhaust his state remedies as required by 28 U.S. Code, 2254 before seeking federal habeas corpus?

Decision: Yes to both questions. Opinion by Justice Brennan. Vote: 6-3.

Reasons: Under *Smith* v. *Hooey,* 393 U.S. 374 (1969), Braden had a constitutional right to force Kentucky to bring him promptly to trial. After making repeated demands for trial to the courts of Kentucky, Braden's demand for a speedy trial was rejected. "Under these circumstances it is clear that [Braden] . . . has exhausted all available state court remedies for consideration of that constitutional claim, even though Kentucky has not brought him to trial."

Regarding the issue of whether the U.S. District Court for Western Kentucky had jurisdiction to hear Braden's habeas corpus petition under 28 U.S. Code, 2241(a), while Braden was incarcerated in Alabama, the Court noted that Kentucky would be a convenient forum because that was where all of the material events took place, and where the records and witnesses pertinent to Braden's claim were likely to be found. Rejecting the contention that its earlier decision in *Ahrens* v. *Clark,* 335 U.S. 188 (1948), had held that section 2241(a) limited a district court's habeas corpus jurisdiction to cases where the prisoner seeking relief is confined within its territorial jurisdiction, the Court reasoned that recent statutory changes expanding the jurisdiction of district courts to hear federal habeas corpus petitions under 28 U.S. Code, 2255 and the broad purposes of the "Great Writ" compelled the conclusion that under section 2241(a) a district court may issue a writ of habeas corpus so long as it has jurisdiction over the state prisoner's custodian. Apparently characterizing the Alabama warden as the agent of Kentucky, the Court thus held that the district court had jurisdiction to hear Braden's habeas corpus petition because his "custodian" (the person against whom he sought relief) was in Kentucky. (Braden at the time of his Kentucky indictment was incarcerated in California. When Kentucky officials originally returned him to Kentucky to stand trial, he escaped to Alabama where he committed new crimes for which he was convicted and incarcerated before seeking a "speedy" trial on his original Kentucky indictment.)

Hensley v. Municipal Court, 411 U.S. 345 (1973)

Facts: After conviction of a crime under California law and release on his own recognizance pending the execution of his sentence, Hensley sought federal habeas corpus relief under 28 U.S. Code, 2254(b) attacking the constitutionality of his conviction. A lower federal court denied relief on the ground that federal habeas corpus is available under section 2254(b) only to persons "in custody pursuant to the judgment of a State court" and that Hensley was not "in custody" within the meaning of that section because he was released on his own recognizance pending execution of his sentence.

Question: Was Hensley "in custody" within the meaning of section 2254(b) thereby entitling him to seek habeas corpus relief?

Decision: Yes. Opinion by Justice Brennan. Vote: 6-3.

Reasons: Under California law, the conditions of Hensley's release on his own recognizance required him to appear at all times and places as ordered by the court which released him and to waive extradition if apprehended outside California after a failure to appear. Further, Hensley's release could be revoked at any time. Prior Supreme Court decisions have interpreted the habeas corpus statute with liberality and flexibility to ensure that miscarriages of justice are surfaced and corrected. "The custody requirement of the habeas corpus statute is designed to preserve the writ of habeas corpus as a remedy for severe restraints on individual liberty." The great purpose of habeas corpus is best served by holding that the restraints on Hensley—the obligation to appear at all times and all places as ordered by any court or be subject to criminal punishment for failure to appear plus the state's express determination to incarcerate him if his habeas corpus petition failed—put Hensley in custody within the meaning of section 2254(b). Moreover, such a holding interfered with no significant state interest because a contrary result would have done no more than postpone this habeas corpus petition until Hensley began serving his sentence.

Preiser v. Rodriguez, 411 U.S. 475 (1973)

Facts: Three state prisoners brought suit in federal court under 42 U.S. Code, 1983 alleging that they were deprived of "good time" credits by state prison officials in violation of their constitutional rights and seeking injunctive relief to compel restoration of the credits which in each case would result in the prisoner's immediate release from confinement. The prison officials contended that the section 1983 action was tantamount to a petition for habeas corpus under 28 U.S. Code, 2254 because the prisoners were seeking release from confinement and thus the prisoners should be required to exhaust their remedies in state court under 28 U.S. Code, 2254(b). (State prisoners seeking federal habeas corpus must first exhaust their state court remedies whereas the general rule regarding state prisoner suits under section 1983 is that exhaustion of state court remedies is not required before suing in federal court. Generally speaking, section 1983 gives state prisoners the right to sue state officials based on a deprivation of con-

60

stitutional rights so that a prisoner's suit often falls within the language of both the federal habeas corpus statute, 28 U.S. Code, 2254, and section 1983.)

Question: Must state prisoners suing under section 1983 who seek immediate release or shortening of confinement exhaust their state court remedies before suing in federal court?

Decision: Yes. Opinion by Justice Stewart. Vote: 6-3.

Reasons: "[T]he essence of habeas corpus is an attack by a person in custody upon the legality of that custody" and the traditional function of a writ of habeas corpus is to secure release from illegal custody. Recent Supreme Court decisions have established that habeas corpus is also available to attack future confinement and obtain future releases. Thus, "even if restoration of . . . [the state prisoners'] good time credits had merely shortened the length of their confinement, rather than required immediate discharge from that confinement, their suits would still have been within the core of habeas corpus in attacking the very duration of their physical confinement itself," and they would be required to exhaust their state court remedies even though their suit was styled under section 1983. The Court reasoned that the purpose of exhaustion in federal habeas corpus was "rooted in considerations of federal-state comity" and that permitting direct federal interference in state prison regulation would stimulate rather than avoid federal-state friction. Significantly, however, the Court specifically reaffirmed several earlier opinions holding that exhaustion is not required when a state prisoner challenges the constitutionality of the conditions of his confinement under section 1983.

The Court's holding leads to the rather inconsistent rule that a state prisoner challenging the constitutionality of certain acts of state officials and seeking injunctive relief that would cause his release or a shortening of his confinement as well as damages for those same acts must proceed first in state court insofar as injunctive relief is sought but can sue directly in federal court insofar as damages are sought. Thus, the likelihood of state and federal courts concurrently determining the constitutionality of the same acts is high with the consequent problems of res judicata or collateral estoppel arising when either the state or federal court decides its case before the other makes its decision.

Tollett v. Henderson, 411 U.S. 258 (1973)

Facts: Having pled guilty to a charge of first degree murder on the advice of counsel and having been sentenced to 99 years' imprisonment, Henderson challenged the constitutionality of his conviction 25 years later in seeking habeas corpus relief on the ground that the indictment to which he pled was returned by an unconstitutionally selected grand jury from which Negroes were systematically excluded. A lower federal court granted Henderson habeas corpus relief, finding that Henderson's grand jury was unconstitutionally selected and concluding that the guilty plea did not waive his right to raise this constitutional issue since his attorney never informed him of his constitutional rights with respect to the composition of a grand jury.

Question: Can a state prisoner who pled guilty with the advice of counsel obtain release through federal habeas corpus by proving only that the indictment to which he pled was returned by an unconstitutionally selected grand jury?

Decision: No. Opinion by Justice Rehnquist. Vote: 6-3.

Reasons: Earlier Supreme Court decisions in *Brady* v. *United States,* 397 U.S. 742 (1970), *McMann* v. *Richardson,* 397 U.S. 770 (1970), and *Parker* v. *North Carolina,* 397 U.S. 790 (1970) stand for the proposition that a defendant's guilty plea forecloses his opportunity to later challenge the constitutionality of acts occurring antecedent to the plea. Thus, Henderson's guilty plea "forecloses independent inquiry into the claim of discrimination in the selection of the grand jury." However, prior cases hold that a guilty plea is valid only if "voluntarily and intelligently entered." Because Henderson pled guilty on the advice of counsel, he can attack the validity of his plea only by showing that the advice he received was not "within the range of competence demanded of attorneys in criminal cases." Because that issue was not properly before it, the Court remanded the case to a lower federal court to determine the validity of Henderson's guilty plea.

Davis v. United States, 411 U.S. 233 (1973)

Facts: A federal prisoner sought habeas corpus relief under 28 U.S. Code, 2255 on the ground that the grand jury that indicted him was unconstitutionally selected thereby rendering his indictment invalid. This objection was not raised by the prisoner at his trial although he had opportunity to do so. A lower federal court denied relief on the ground that the prisoner had waived his right to assert such a claim under rule 12(b)(2) of the Federal Rules of Criminal Procedure (FRCP) which provides that "[d]efenses and objections based on defects in the institution of the prosecution or in the indictment . . . may be raised only before trial" and that failure to present such defenses or objections "constitutes a waiver thereof" unless for "cause shown" the court grants relief from the waiver. The prisoner contended that he should be permitted to contest the constitutionality of his indictment unless a hearing was held at which it was established that he had "deliberately bypassed" or "understandingly and knowingly" waived his claim of unconstitutional grand jury selection under the standards set forth in *Fay* v. *Noia,* 372 U.S. 391 (1963) and *Johnson* v. *Zerbst,* 304 U.S. 458 (1938).

Question: Can a defendant who waived his right to raise a claim at trial under rule 12(b)(2) of the FRCP nevertheless raise that claim in seeking federal habeas corpus relief unless it is shown that he knowingly and understandingly failed to raise that claim at trial?

Decision: No. Opinion by Justice Rehnquist. Vote: 6-3.

Reasons: The purpose of the waiver provisions of rule 12(b)(2) is to force claims of defects in the institution of criminal proceedings to be made before trial so that such defects may be cured before the court, the witnesses, and the parties have gone to the burden and expense of a trial. In accord with this purpose, the Court held in *Shotwell Mfg. Co.* v. *United States,* 371 U.S. 341 (1963), that failure to timely assert a constitutional challenge to the grand jury array under rule 12(b)(2) precluded raising such claim on direct appeal. In *Kaufman* v. *United States,* 394 U.S. 217 (1969), however, the Court in effect held that, at least in the absence of a federal statute expressly forbidding it, a federal prisoner seeking habeas corpus relief could raise any constitutional claim whether or not raised at trial unless the prisoner had "understandably and knowingly" waived that claim.

Justice Rehnquist speaking for the Court concluded that constitutional claims barred by the express waiver provisions in rule 12(b)(2) could not be raised on habeas corpus relief notwithstanding the general rule established in *Kaufman* that all constitutional claims may be raised in habeas corpus unless knowingly and understandably waived because "it [is] inconceivable that Congress, having in the criminal proceeding foreclosed the raising of a claim . . . after the commencement of trial in the absence of a showing of 'cause' for relief from waiver, nonetheless intended to perversely negate the Rule's purpose by permitting an entirely different but much more liberal requirement of waiver in federal habeas proceedings." The Court thus held that "the waiver standard expressed in Rule 12(b)(2) governs an untimely claim of grand jury discrimination, not only during the criminal proceeding, but also later in collateral review."

Murch v. *Mottram,* 409 U.S. 41 (1972)

Facts: The defendant, convicted in 1960 of larceny and as a habitual offender, declined to litigate certain constitutional issues on direct appeal when his convictions were upheld. After the defendant's 1963 grant of parole was revoked, he sued in state court to set aside the parole revocation, but declined to challenge the constitutionality of his underlying conviction after the state judge warned him that failure to do so would constitute a waiver of his right to challenge his conviction later on constitutional grounds. (The defendant consulted with his lawyer before making his choice not to challenge his underlying conviction.) After an unsuccessful attack on his parole revocation in state court, the defendant was ultimately granted habeas corpus in a lower federal court which set aside his conviction on the same constitutional grounds he had refused to present to state courts, either on direct appeal from his conviction or in his suit attacking his parole revocation.

Question: Did the lower federal court err in granting the defendant habeas corpus relief because by failing properly to challenge his conviction in state courts he waived his right to present those constitutional claims in federal courts?

Decision: Yes. Per curiam opinion. Vote: 6-3.

Reasons: In *Fay* v. *Noia,* 372 U.S. 391 (1963), the Court stated that a federal court could deny habeas corpus relief to any applicant who knowingly, after consultation with counsel or otherwise, deliberately bypassed available state procedures for presenting his federal claims in state courts. In *Sanders* v. *United States,* 373 U.S. 1 (1963), the Court stated that in order to prevent piecemeal litigation and endless delay any prisoner who "deliberately withholds one of two grounds for federal collateral [habeas corpus] relief at the time of filing his first application in the hope of being granted two hearings rather than one or for some other such reason, . . . may be deemed to have waived his right to a hearing on a second application presenting the withheld ground." Reasoning that the state procedure in this case was reasonable in requiring prisoners seeking postconviction relief to assert all known constitutional claims in a single proceeding and that the defendant deliberately bypassed his opportunity to present his constitutional claims to state courts, the Court concluded that under *Fay* v. *Noia* the defendant waived his right to present his constitutional claims to federal courts and thus the lower federal court erred in granting him habeas corpus relief.

Swenson v. Stidham, 409 U.S. 224 (1972)

Facts: During his Missouri state trial and conviction of first-degree murder in 1955, Stidham challenged the admissibility into evidence of his confession on the ground that it was involuntary. Out of the presence of the jury, the trial judge seemingly determined that the confession was admissible and voluntary. In subsequent state court proceedings, the Missouri Supreme Court upheld a determination that Stidham's confession was voluntary and that the trial judge had properly met the constitutional requirements set forth in *Jackson* v. *Denno,* 378 U.S. 368 (1964), which held that before a jury could constitutionally hear a confession, the trial judge must independently determine out of the jury's presence whether the confession was voluntary. After Stidham sought habeas corpus relief on the ground that the state trial judge failed to comply with the mandates of *Jackson* v. *Denno,* a lower federal court held that Stidham was entitled to a new hearing in state court on whether his confession was voluntary.

Question: Did the lower federal court err in granting Stidham a new hearing on the issue of whether his confession was voluntary?

Decision: Yes. Opinion by Justice White. Vote: 9-0.

Reasons: "Even if the trial procedure was flawed with respect to the challenged confession, *Jackson* v. *Denno* does not entitle Stidham to a new trial if the State subsequently provided him an error-free judicial determination of the voluntariness of his confession—error-free in that the determination was procedurally adequate and substantively acceptable under the Due Process Clause. . . . Here, the Missouri courts, in connection with Stidham's second motion to vacate his sentence, unquestionably furnished a procedurally adequate evidentiary hearing and the outcome was adverse to Stidham." The Court noted, however, that Stidham was still free in a habeas corpus proceeding to raise in federal court the claim that the state court erred in determining that his confession was voluntary.

La Vallee v. Delle Rose, 410 U.S. 690 (1973)

Facts: In a petition for a writ of habeas corpus in lower federal court, a state prisoner convicted of murder under state law claimed that his conviction was invalid because his confessions were admitted in evidence against him at trial even though they were involuntary in violation of the Fifth Amendment. (The Supreme Court has long held that the introduction of a defendant's involuntary statement at his criminal trial is unconstitutional.) Under 28 U.S. Code, 2254(d), when a state prisoner seeks habeas corpus in federal court, any state court findings that have been adequately determined are presumed to be correct and the prisoner has the burden of establishing by convincing evidence that a state court's conclusion was erroneous. Lower federal courts refused to give the state court finding, that the prisoner's challenged confession was voluntary, a presumption of correctness under section 2254(d) because they concluded the state court opinion did not specifically resolve issues of credibility against the prisoner.

Question: Was the state court's finding that the prisoner's challenged confession was voluntary entitled under section 2254(d) to a presumption of correctness because it was adequately and reliably determined?

Decision: Yes. Per curiam opinion. Vote: 5-4.

Reasons: After extensively summarizing the trial evidence and the defendant's explanation of certain of his confession statements, the state court concluded:

> On all evidence, both at the trial and at the hearing, and after considering the totality of the circumstances, including the omission to warn defendant of his right to counsel and his right against self-incrimination, I find and decide that the respective confessions to the police and district attorney were, in all respects, voluntary and legally admissible in evidence at the trial. . . .

The Supreme Court concluded that, "Although it is true that the state trial court did not specifically articulate its credibility findings, it can scarcely be doubted from its written opinion that . . . [defendant's] factual contentions were resolved against him."

In *Townsend* v. *Sain,* 372 U.S. 293 (1963), the Court set forth general standards governing the holding of hearings on federal habeas corpus petitions, stating:

> [T]he possibility of legal error may be eliminated in many situations if the fact finder has articulated the constitutional standards which he has applied. Furthermore, the coequal responsibilities of state and federal judges in the administration of federal constitutional law are such that we think the district judge may, in the ordinary case in which there has been no articulation, properly assume that the state trier of fact applied correct standards of federal law to the facts, in the absence of evidence . . . that there is reason to suspect that an incorrect standard was applied. Thus, if third-degree methods of obtaining a confession are

alleged and the state court refused to exclude the confession from evidence, the district judge may assume that the state trier found the facts against the petitioner, the law being, of course, that third-degree methods necessarily produce a coerced confession.

Concluding that the state court applied proper constitutional standards in determining that the challenged confession was voluntary, the Court held that this state court finding was entitled to a presumption of correctness under section 2254(d).

Neil v. *Biggers*, 409 U.S. 188 (1972)

Facts: During defendant's trial in a Tennessee court in which he was convicted of rape, the alleged victim testified to an identification she made of the defendant at a police station. The identification occurred after two detectives walked the defendant past the victim and the defendant was directed to say, "Shut up or I'll kill you." After the Tennessee Supreme Court affirmed the defendant's conviction, the U.S. Supreme Court granted certiorari and affirmed the judgment of the Tennessee Supreme Court by an equally divided court (4-4 vote). The defendant then sought federal habeas corpus relief on the ground that his conviction was unconstitutional because the station house identification procedure (by which the rape victim identified the defendant) was so suggestive as to violate due process. Although these grounds for relief were previously asserted before the U.S. Supreme Court which affirmed the defendant's conviction, a lower federal court set aside the defendant's conviction, notwithstanding 28 U.S. Code, 2244(c) which provides that issues actually adjudicated by the Supreme Court may not be reopened in habeas corpus.

Questions: Did the lower federal court err in adjudicating the defendant's habeas corpus claim which had previously been decided by an equally divided Supreme Court? Did the lower federal court err in concluding that the station house identification procedure used to identify the defendant was so suggestive as to violate due process?

Decision: No to the first question and yes to the second. Opinion by Justice Powell. Vote: 8-0 on the first question and 5-3 on the second question.

Reasons: Federal habeas corpus is designed to permit state prisoners to litigate their constitutional claims at least once in a federal court, and 28 U.S. Code, 2244(c) recognizes this purpose by precluding relitigation of claims which a state prisoner has "actually litigated" before the U.S. Supreme Court. However, when the Supreme Court affirms a lower court judgment by an equally divided court, its decision is entitled to no precedential weight, and it has not "actually litigated" the merits of the claims presented for purposes of section 2244(c).

Turning to the second question, the Court found that the extensive and intimate contact which the rape victim had with the defendant prior to her station house identification made the likelihood of misidentification small. In *Stovall* v. *Denno,* 388 U.S. 293 (1967), the Court held that a defendant whose identification was the product of a confrontation that was "unnecessarily suggestive and conducive to irreparable mistaken identification" denied him due process. In the totality of circumstances in this case, considering the rape victim's opportunity to view the defendant at the time of the crime, the length of time between the crime and the challenged station house identification, and the victim's certainty of the defendant's identity, the Court concluded that the challenged identification was reliable and thus did not violate due process under the mandate of *Stovall* v. *Denno*. The Court specifically rejected the argument that the identification testimony should have been excluded solely because the identification procedures were unnecessarily suggestive in that the police did not exhaust all possibilities in seeking persons physically comparable to the defendant in order to construct a suitable line-up.

Gosa v. Mayden, 413 U.S. 665 (1973)

Facts: In *O'Callahan* v. *Parker,* 395 U.S. 258 (1969), the Court held that a serviceman charged with crime can constitutionally be tried by a military tribunal only if the crime is "service connected." Two servicemen convicted of crimes by military tribunals before the decision in *O'Callahan* sought habeas corpus relief on the ground that the ruling in *O'Callahan* was retroactive and their crimes were not "service connected."

Question: Is *O'Callahan* v. *Parker* retroactive?

Decision: No. Opinion by Justice Blackmun. Vote: 5-4.

Reasons: Whether *O'Callahan* should be accorded retroactive effect should be determined by analyzing: (1) the purpose to be served by the new constitutional standard, (2) the extent of reliance by law enforcement authorities on old standards, and (3) the effect on the administration of justice of a retroactive application of the new standard. If the purpose of a new constitutional procedural standard is to overcome substantial deficiencies in the truth-finding process, then retroactivity is mandated. *O'Callahan*, however, although not uncritical of the military system of justice in stressing possible command influence and the lack of certain procedural safeguards, was not based on any finding that the court-martial lacks fundamental integrity in its truth-determining process. Regarding reliance, before *O'Callahan* the law was settled that the exercise of military jurisdiction over an offense allegedly committed by a member of the armed forces was appropriately based on the military status of the defendant. The military justifiably relied on this settled law prior to *O'Callahan*. Lastly, the Court concluded that retroactivity would substantially disrupt the administration of justice by opening to possible attack all courts-martial since 1916 on the basis of stale records. This would affect not only the validity of criminal convictions but adjustments in back pay, veterans' benefits, retirement pay, pensions, and other matters. "[T]he purpose to be served by *O'Callahan,* the reliance on the law as it stood before that decision and the effect of a holding of retroactivity all require that *O'Callahan* be accorded prospective application only."

Michigan v. Payne, 412 U.S. 47 (1973)

Facts: After pleading guilty to a charge of assault with intent to commit murder and receiving sentence, the defendant had his guilty plea invalidated, was tried and convicted by a jury, and received a higher sentence by the resentencing judge on March 30, 1967, in violation of the resentencing procedures later constitutionally mandated in *North Carolina* v. *Pearce,* 395 U.S. 711 (1969). *Pearce* held that a resentencing judge in such circumstances must state the reasons for the harsher sentence and such reasons must be based upon the defendant's conduct occurring after the original sentencing.

Question: Should *North Carolina* v. *Pearce* be given retroactive effect?

Decision: No. Opinion by Justice Powell. Vote: 6-3.

Reasons: Three criteria should be considered in determining whether constitutional protections in the area of criminal procedure are to be applied retroactively: "(a) the purpose to be served by the new standards, (b) the extent of the reliance by law enforcement authorities on the old standards, and (c) the effect on the administration of justice of a retroactive application of the new standards. . . . The two purposes for the resentencing restrictions imposed by *Pearce* were to ensure (i) 'that vindictiveness against a defendant for having successfully attacked his first conviction . . .' would 'play no part in the sentence he receives after a new trial . . .' and (ii) that apprehension of such vindictiveness would not 'deter a defendant's exercise of the right to appeal or collaterally attack his first conviction. . . .'" The latter purpose is of no consequence in determining the issue of retroactivity because *Pearce* clearly did not contemplate that every defendant who had not appealed prior to *Pearce* would have his opportunity to appeal revived. The other purpose of *Pearce* was to prevent possible vindictive sentencing, even though most judges would not be vindictive. Nonretroactive application of *Pearce* would not preclude defendants from overturning harsher resentencing upon proof of actual vindictiveness, whereas retroactive application would permit a windfall to defendants who were resentenced without actual vindictiveness. The Court thus concluded that the purposes of *Pearce* favored nonretroactive application.

The Court also concluded that the two other factors—reliance and burden on the administration of justice—favored nonretroactivity because the holding of *Pearce* was not foreshadowed by prior Supreme Court decisions and because resentencing defendants under *Pearce* standards "would present considerable difficulties, since judges like witnesses in criminal trials, lack infallible memories and perfect records of their motivations."

Chaffin v. Stynchcombe, 412 U.S. 17 (1973)

Facts: Upon retrial following the reversal of his earlier conviction, the defendant was again found guilty and sentenced by the jury to a greater term than had been imposed by the first jury. The defendant challenged the constitutionality of his conviction and sentence on grounds that the rendition of a higher sentence by a jury upon retrial violated: (1) the Double Jeopardy Clause, (2) the Due Process Clause by permitting vindictiveness in the second jury sentencing, and (3) the defendant's right to appeal without fearing a higher sentence upon retrial.

Question: May states that entrust the sentencing responsibility to the jury constitutionally permit higher sentences by juries on retrials following reversals of prior convictions?

Decision: Yes. Opinion by Justice Powell. Vote: 5-4.

Reasons: Prior case law clearly holds that the Double Jeopardy Clause is not violated when at the behest of the defendant a criminal conviction is set aside, a new trial ordered, and the defendant receives a harsher sentence upon retrial. Declining to overturn this well-established constitutional principle, the Court rejected the defendant's double jeopardy claim.

The Court also rejected the defendant's factual contention that a second jury would be vindictive after retrial and thereby unconstitutionally punish persons who successfully exercised their right to appeal. In *North Carolina* v. *Pearce,* 395 U.S. 711 (1969), the Court held that in order to prevent a judge from vindictively imposing a greater sentence on a defendant who had successfully attacked his conviction, the judge's reasons for the harsher sentence must be affirmatively stated and be based upon "objective information concerning identifiable conduct on the part of the defendant occurring after the time of the original sentencing proceeding." The *Pearce* rule was premised on the fact that judges would resent having their decisions overturned. In this case, however, the re-sentencing jury had no knowledge of defendant's prior conviction, had no personal stake in the prior conviction, and would otherwise have no reason to be vindictive in its sentencing. The Court thus concluded that the *Pearce* rationale was inapplicable to resentencing by juries.

Turning to the claim that harsher sentences on retrial are always unconstitutional because they have a "chilling effect" on a defendant's right to challenge his conviction on direct appeal or habeas corpus, the Court concluded that harsher sentences in such circumstances were permissible to serve the valid state interest of giving juries broad sentencing discretion. The Court also deemed any chilling effect on appeals to be insubstantial because "the likelihood of actually receiving a harsher sentence is quite remote at the time a convicted defendant begins to question whether he will appeal."

Robinson v. Neil, 409 U.S. 505 (1973)

Facts: After being tried and convicted in the Chattanooga, Tennessee, municipal court for violating the city ordinance which prohibits assault and battery, petitioner later pled guilty to a charge of assault with intent to commit murder in violation of state law. The state charge grew out of the same circumstances that gave rise to petitioner's municipal trial. After the subsequent Supreme Court decisions in *Benton* v. *Maryland,* 395 U.S. 784 (1969), and *Waller* v. *Florida,*

69

397 U.S. 387 (1970), holding that the Fifth Amendment's protection against double jeopardy was binding upon the states through the Fourteenth Amendment and that this protection prohibited the prosecution of persons in state and municipal courts for the same offense, the petitioner sought habeas corpus relief on the ground that his conviction in state court violated the constitutional prohibition against double jeopardy.

Question: Should the Court's decision in *Waller* v. *Florida* prohibiting state and municipal prosecutions for the same offense be applied retroactively?

Decision: Yes. Opinion by Justice Rehnquist. Vote: 9-0.

Reasons: In *Linkletter* v. *Walker,* 381 U.S. 618 (1965), the Court held that with respect to new constitutional interpretations involving criminal rights, "the Constitution neither prohibits nor requires retrospective effect." *Linkletter* and later Supreme Court cases suggested that only those new criminal constitutional protections affecting "the very integrity of the fact-finding process" would be given retrospective effect. The Court concluded in this case that the *Linkletter* analysis was generally inapplicable to determining the retroactivity of *Waller,* which absolutely prohibited a second trial whether or not the fact-finding process in the first trial passed constitutional muster. The Court also observed that retroactive application of *Waller* would minimally disrupt the administration of criminal justice and that *Waller* did not mark a departure from past decisions of the Court, and thus held that *Waller* should be accorded full retroactive effect.

Illinois v. Somerville, 410 U.S. 458 (1973)

Facts: After Somerville was indicted by an Illinois grand jury for theft, his case called to trial and a jury impaneled and sworn, but before any evidence was taken, the trial judge granted the state's motion for a mistrial on the ground that the indictment was fatally deficient under Illinois law because it failed to allege that Somerville intended to permanently deprive the owner of his property, a necessary element to the crime of theft. Under Illinois law, the defect in the indictment was "jurisdictional"—it could not be waived by the defendant's failure to object and could be asserted on appeal or in a post-conviction proceeding to overturn a final judgment of conviction. After the grand jury handed down a second indictment a short time later, which alleged the requisite intent, Somerville was tried and convicted of theft over his claim that the second trial was barred by the Fifth Amendment prohibition against double jeopardy.

Question: Was Somerville's second trial for theft after the first case was dismissed at the state's instance because of a defect in the grand jury indictment barred by the Fifth Amendment prohibition against double jeopardy?

Decision: No. Opinion by Justice Rehnquist. Vote: 5-4.

Reasons: Past Supreme Court decisions have followed the rule that a second trial of a criminal defendant after a mistrial is not constitutionally barred by the Fifth Amendment if "in the context of that particular [first] trial, the declaration of a mistrial was dictated by 'manifest necessity' or the 'ends of public justice'. . . . This formulation . . . abjures the application of any mechanical formula by which to judge the propriety of declaring a mistrial in the varying and often unique situations arising in the course of a criminal trial." To serve the "ends of public justice," a trial judge may properly declare a mistrial if an impartial verdict cannot be reached or if a conviction would have to be reversed on appeal due to an obvious procedural error in the trial. Reasoning in the instant case that a mistrial was declared because the defective grand jury indictment, not curable by amendment, would have invalidated any conviction of Somerville under Illinois law and that the state did not take advantage of the mistrial to increase the chances of conviction, the Court concluded that Somerville's second trial did not constitute double jeopardy because the mistrial was declared to serve the ends of public justice. (Illinois forbade amendments to defective indictments in order to preserve a criminal defendant's right under Illinois law to have all actions against him commenced by the action of a grand jury.) "[W]here the declaration of a mistrial implements a reasonable state policy and aborts a proceeding that at best would have produced a verdict that could have been upset at will by one of the parties, the defendant's interest in proceeding to verdict is outweighed by the competing and equally legitimate demand for public justice."

One Lot Emerald Cut Stones v. *United States*, 409 U.S. 232 (1973)

Facts: Francis Klementova was indicted, tried, and acquitted of charges that he violated 18 U.S. Code, 545 by willfully and knowingly, with intent to defraud the United States, smuggling one lot of emerald cut stones and one ring into the United States without submitting to the required customs procedures. Following the acquittal, the government sought to recover the emerald stones and ring under 19 U.S. Code, 1497 which provides for the forfeiture of all articles passing through customs "not [properly] included in the declaration and entry as made . . ." and imposes a monetary penalty equal to the value of such articles upon their possessor. Klementova contended the forfeiture proceeding was barred by the doctrine of collateral estoppel and the Fifth Amendment prohibition against double jeopardy.

Question: Is the government's forfeiture proceeding against the emerald stones and ring under 19 U.S. Code, 1497 barred either by collateral estoppel or the Fifth Amendment prohibition against double jeopardy?

Decision: No. Per curiam opinion. Vote: 9-0.

Reasons: "Collateral estoppel would bar a forfeiture under section 1497 if, in the earlier criminal proceeding [under 18 U.S. Code, 545], the elements of a section 1497 forfeiture had been resolved against the Government." However, the government must prove criminal intent in section 545 prosecutions and must prove each element of its case beyond a reasonable doubt, whereas in section 1497 civil forfeiture proceedings criminal intent is irrelevant and the government must prove its case only by a preponderance of the evidence. Thus, Klementova's acquittal on the section 545 criminal charges did not necessarily resolve the issues in the section 1497 civil forfeiture suit so that the government is not barred from maintaining that suit by collateral estoppel.

Since the Double Jeopardy Clause prohibits two criminal punishments or two attempts to punish for the same offense but does not prohibit the imposition of both a criminal and civil sanction for the same act or omission, the Court held that the challenged civil forfeiture proceeding was not barred by Klementova's prior acquittal of criminal charges under section 545. The Court characterized the forfeiture of articles under section 1497 as a civil sanction because: (1) it aided in the enforcement of tariff regulations, (2) the monetary penalty imposed was not excessive and served to reimburse the government for investigation and enforcement expenses, and (3) Congress did not intend section 1497 to be punitive but only remedial. The Court thus concluded that the "Section 1497 forfeiture is civil and remedial, and, as a result, its imposition is not barred by an acquittal of charges of violating Section 545."

McGinnis v. Royster, 410 U.S. 263 (1973)

Facts: A New York statute denied state prisoners "good time" credit for pre-sentence incarceration in county jails. It operated so as to permit state prisoners who were free on bail before trial to obtain parole earlier than pre-sentence detainees when the total number of days incarcerated, pre-trial as well as post-conviction, were considered. New York law granted good time credit for pre-sentence incarceration to those prisoners ultimately sentenced to county penitentiaries, however, as opposed to those convicted of felonies who were sentenced to state prison.

Question: Does the New York statute violate equal protection of the laws and discriminate against those state prisoners unable to afford or otherwise qualify for bail prior to trial because it denies state prisoners good time credit for pre-sentence incarceration but permits those prisoners who obtain bail immediately to receive good time credit for the entire period which they ultimately spend in custody?

Decision: No. Opinion by Justice Powell. Vote: 7-2.

Reasons: Statutes determining a minimum time for parole eligibility need only a rational basis to sustain them against challenge on equal protection grounds. The good time provision of the challenged New York law was intended to encourage state prisoners to engage in rehabilitation courses and activities which exist only in state prisons and not in county jails. Also, a prisoner's conduct and performance are evaluated and scrutinized in state prisons as they are not in county jails (where most prisoners are awaiting trial). Therefore, the Court concluded that there was a rational basis for declining to give good time credit for pre-sentence incarceration in county jails "[w]here there is no evaluation by state officials and little or no rehabilitation for anyone to evaluate. . . ." Giving county penitentiary inmates, who were nonfelons serving less than one-year sentences good time credit for pre-sentence jail time while denying it to state prisoner felons was also held constitutional because the legislature might rationally conclude that the risk of misevaluating nonfelons was less than the risk of misevaluating those convicted of more serious crimes.

Hurtado v. United States, 410 U.S. 578 (1973)

Facts: Unable to make bail, Mexican citizens (petitioners) were incarcerated under rule 46(b) of the Federal Rules of Criminal Procedure to assure their presence at the trials of those accused of illegally bringing them into the United States. During their incarceration, the petitioners were paid $1 for every day of their confinement plus $20 for each day they attended court under 28 U.S. Code, 1821 which provides a "witness attending in any court of the United States . . . shall receive $20 for each day's attendance and for the time necessarily occupied in going to and returning from the same . . ." and which also entitles "a witness . . . detained in prison for want of security for his appearance, . . . in addition to his subsistence, to a compensation of $1 per day." The petitioners contended that section 1821, properly interpreted, entitled them to $20 in witness fees every day they were incarcerated, and if it was not so interpreted, the statute violated due process and equal protection by invidiously discriminating against those too poor to afford bail.

Questions: Does section 1821 entitle witnesses incarcerated for want of security to a $20 fee for each day of incarceration? If not, is section 1821 unconstitutional in violation of equal protection and due process?

Decision: No to both questions. Opinion by Justice Stewart. Vote: 7-2.

Reasons: Under section 1821, a witness is "eligible for the $20 fee only when two requirements are satisfied—when there is a court in session that he is to attend, and when he is in necessary attendance on that court." Thus, the incarcerated petitioners were entitled to the $20 compensation for every day of confinement during the trial or other proceeding for which they had been detained. (Because a court may not call a case to trial for weeks or months, a witness may be incarcerated for a lengthy period without being entitled to the $20 witness fee.)

Rejecting the argument that section 1821 as so construed "took" the incarcerated petitioners' property without just compensation, the Court reasoned that "the Fifth Amendment does not require that the Government pay for the performance of a public duty it is already owed. . . . It is beyond dispute that there is in fact a public obligation to provide evidence . . . no matter how financially burdensome it may be." The Court also concluded that section 1821 did not violate equal protection by "distinguishing the compensation paid for pre-trial detention from the fees paid for attendance at trial." Although section 1821 provides little *pre-trial* compensation to incarcerated witnesses, the government must bear the cost of their food, lodging, and security. "Congress could thus reasonably determine that while some compensation should be provided during the pre-trial detention period, a minimal amount was justified, particularly in view of the fact that the witness has a public duty to testify."

United States v. Bishop, 412 U.S. 346 (1973)

Facts: Charged with willfully making and subscribing to tax returns he did not believe were true in all material matters, a felony under section 7206(1) of the Internal Revenue Code, the defendant unsuccessfully requested the trial judge to instruct the jury that they could properly convict him of a lesser-included-offense, constituting a misdemeanor under section 7207 of the code, if his willfulness was somewhat less than that required for the section 7206(1) felony offense.

Question: Did the trial judge properly refuse the lesser-included-offense instruction because the degree of willfulness necessary to convict under both sections 7206(1) and 7207 is the same?

Decision: Yes. Opinion by Justice Blackmun. Vote: 8-1.

Reasons: The defendant would have been entitled to a lesser-included-offense instruction only if the word "willfully" in the tax felony statute has a meaning more stringent than in the tax misdemeanor statute. (Under the Federal Rules of Criminal Procedure, Rule 31(c), a defendant is entitled to a lesser-included-offense charge if the evidence would permit a jury rationally to find him guilty of the lesser offense and acquit him of the greater.) A review of case law interpreting the word "willfully" in tax felony and tax misdemeanor statutes and the general interchangeability with which Congress has used willfulness in the Internal Revenue Code in connection with felony and misdemeanor statutes compels the conclusion that willfulness has the same meaning in tax misdemeanor statutes that it has in tax felony statutes. That meaning is "bad faith or evil intent" as described in *United States* v. *Murdock,* 290 U.S. 389 (1933).

Keeble v. United States, 412 U.S. 205 (1973)

Facts: The Major Crimes Act of 1885 (Act) authorizes federal courts to try Indians charged with assault with intent to commit serious bodily injury while on an Indian reservation but does not give federal courts jurisdiction to try Indians charged with simple assault. A lower federal court refused to instruct a jury that an Indian on trial for assault with intent to commit serious bodily injury could be found guilty of the lesser-included-offense of simple assault, if the facts so warranted, on the ground that it had no jurisdiction to convict the Indian of simple assault. After conviction, the defendant Indian appealed, claiming that the trial judge's failure to give the lesser-included-offense instruction was reversible error.

Question: Did the trial judge err in failing to instruct the jury that the accused Indian could be found guilty of the lesser-included-offense of simple assault?

Decision: Yes. Opinion by Justice Brennan. Vote: 6-3.

Reasons: Federal Criminal Rule 31(c) entitles a defendant to an instruc-

74

tion on a lesser-included-offense "if the evidence would permit a jury rationally to find him guilty of the lesser offense and acquit him of the greater." When Congress passed the Act extending federal jurisdiction to crimes committed by Indians on Indian land, it expressly provided that Indians be tried *"in the same manner,* as are all other persons" committing the crimes set forth in the Act. The Court thus held that "where an Indian is prosecuted in federal court under the provisions of the Act, the Act does not require that he be deprived of the protection afforded by an instruction on a lesser included offense" if the evidence so warrants.

Bronston v. United States, 409 U.S. 352 (1973)

Facts: During a hearing to determine whether the bankrupt, Bronston Production, Inc., had any "hidden" assets, a lawyer for a creditor of the bankrupt asked its sole owner, Samuel Bronston, whether he personally had ever had any Swiss bank accounts. In response, Mr. Bronston answered truthfully but evasively, "The company had an account there, for about six months in Zurich." Bronston was subsequently convicted for this response under the federal perjury statute, 18 U.S. Code, 1621, for willfully stating a "matter he [did] not believe to be true," on the theory that Bronston himself undisputedly had had Swiss bank accounts in the past and that his answer to the question was a lie by negative implication.

Question: Can a witness be convicted of perjury under 18 U.S. Code, 1621 for an answer, under oath, that is literally true but not responsive to the question asked and arguably misleading by negative implication?

Decision: No. Opinion by Chief Justice Burger. Vote: 9-0.

Reasons: The federal perjury statute confines the offense to the witness who "willfully . . . states any material matter which he does not believe to be true." Although agreeing that Bronston's literally true answer to the crucial question was unresponsive and tended to mislead, the Court nevertheless concluded that Congress did not intend "the drastic sanction of a perjury prosecution to cure a testimonial mishap which could readily have been reached with a single additional question by counsel alert—as every examiner ought to be—to the incongruity of . . . [Bronston's] unresponsive answer. . . . [A]ny special problems arising from the literally true but unresponsive answer are to be remedied through the 'questioner's acuity' and not by a federal perjury prosecution."

United States v. Enmons, 410 U.S. 396 (1973)

Facts: The Hobbs Act, 18 U.S. Code, 1951 makes obstruction of interstate commerce by extortion (defined as obtaining another's property by wrongful use of actual or threatened force or violence) a federal crime punishable by a $10,000 fine and 20 years' imprisonment. While on strike and seeking a new collective-bargaining agreement with the Gulf States Utilities Company (Company), labor union members and officials allegedly conspired to commit five acts of violence, including firing high-powered rifles at three Company transformers, to obtain higher wages and other employment benefits from the Company. For these acts of violence, the union members and officials were charged with violating the Hobbs Act on the theory that they wrongfully used force to obtain the Company's property in the form of higher wages. A lower federal court dismissed the charges on the ground that the Hobbs Act did not forbid the use of force to obtain legitimate union objectives such as higher wages.

Question: Does the Hobbs Act prohibit the alleged acts of violence by the union members and officials during a strike which is intended to obtain higher wages from the Company?

Decision: No. Opinion by Justice Stewart. Vote: 5-4.

Reasons: After tracing the legislative history of the Hobbs Act, the Court concluded that it "does not apply to the use of force to achieve legitimate labor ends." The Hobbs Act was enacted in response to the decision in *United States* v. *Local 807,* 315 U.S. 521 (1942) in which the Court held that a federal criminal anti-racketeering statute did not prohibit New York City Teamsters from lying in wait for out-of-town trucks and demanding payment from their owners or drivers in return for unwanted services and for allowing the trucks to proceed into the city. The congressional response to the *Local 807* case, the Court reasoned, was to make federally punishable under the Hobbs Act those union acts of violence intended to exact payments from employers for imposed, unwanted, and super-fluous services, but not union acts intended to exact payments from employers for desired services furnished pursuant to a collective-bargaining agreement. The Court noted that if the Hobbs Act prohibited the wrongful use of force to obtain the legitimate union demands of higher wages, a worker who threw a punch on a picket line during an economic strike would be subject to a Hobbs Act prosecution and the possibility of 20 years' imprisonment and a $10,000 fine. Two related reasons compelled the rejection of this broad construction of the Hobbs Act: (1) criminal statutes must be strictly construed and any ambiguities resolved in favor of lenity, and (2) such a construction would create an unprecedented federal incursion into the states' criminal jurisdiction by putting the federal government in the position of policing the orderly conduct of strikes.

Federal Courts and Procedure

The Court's most important work in this field concerned issues of standing, justiciability, and the right to a 12-man jury trial in civil cases.

In an important standing case, the Court held that the mother of an illegitimate child lacked standing to challenge the constitutionality of the administration of a criminal child support statute. On the other hand, the Court ruled that citizens alleging injury to the environment had standing to challenge an increase in railroad freight rates for recyclable material. (The summary of this case appears in the administrative law section.)

In a suit growing out of the disorders at Kent State University in 1970, the Court held that a request for continued judicial surveillance over National Guard actions presented a nonjusticiable controversy. The decision tended to indicate that the Court would rule nonjusticiable any challenges to the constitutionality of continuing United States involvement in Vietnam, Cambodia, and Laos.

The Court also upheld the constitutionality of six-man jury trials in federal civil cases, finding that such juries produced results no different from twelve-member juries.

Linda R. S. v. Richard D., 410 U.S. 614 (1973)

Facts: The mother of an illegitimate child brought suit to enjoin the discriminatory application of a Texas criminal statute making it unlawful for "any parent" to refuse to support his children. The Texas courts had construed the statute to apply solely to the parents of legitimate children and to impose no duty of support on the parents of illegitimate children. The district court dismissed the suit on the ground that the mother had an insufficient stake in the outcome of the controversy to confer standing to challenge the Texas penal statute.

Question: Did the mother of an illegitimate child lack standing to challenge the constitutionality of the administration of the Texas criminal child support statute?

Decision: Yes. Opinion by Justice Marshall. Vote: 5-4.

Reasons: To confer standing, the mother must allege "such a personal stake in the outcome of the controversy as to assure that concrete adverseness which sharpens the presentation of issues upon which the court so largely depends for illumination of difficult constitutional questions. . . . The party who invokes [judicial] power must be able to show . . . that he has sustained or is immediately in danger of sustaining some direct injury as the result of [a statute's] enforcement." In this case, the mother failed to show that her inability to secure support payments resulted from the nonenforcement of the challenged Texas penal statute against her child's father. Moreover, the prospect that prosecution of the father under that statute will result in future payment of support "can, at best, be termed only speculative. . . . [T]he 'direct' relationship between the alleged injury and the claim sought to be adjudicated, which previous decisions of this Court suggest is a prerequisite of standing, is absent in this case."

Justice White, in a dissenting opinion, noted that it was odd for the majority to conclude that the effect of enforcing the Texas criminal child support statute against the father was only speculative in light of the widespread assumption that the threat of penal sanctions has "something more than a 'speculative' effect on a person's conduct."

Gilligan v. Morgan, 413 U.S. 1 (1973)

Facts: Certain students who attended Kent State University during the period of civil disorder on campus in May 1970, sought injunctive relief against the Governor of Ohio to prevent the improper use of National Guard troops to quell civil disorders. The students sought continuing judicial surveillance over the Ohio

National Guard to assure compliance with newly changed standards concerning training, weaponing, and orders. A lower federal court dismissed the suit on the ground that it presented a nonjusticiable controversy beyond the scope of judicial authority.

Question: Did the suit seeking continued judicial surveillance over the National Guard present a nonjusticiable controversy?

Decision: Yes. Opinion by Chief Justice Burger. Vote: 5-4.

Reasons: Justiciability is not a legal concept with a fixed content. Generally speaking, no justiciable controversy is presented when the question sought to be adjudicated is political, moot, advisory in nature, or when the parties lack standing to maintain the suit. In this case, most of the issues raised in the original suit are moot, none of the student plaintiffs are now enrolled at Kent State, and the judicial relief sought is advisory in nature. Moreover, Article I, Section 8, clause 16 of the Constitution expressly vests Congress with power to prescribe the methods for organizing, arming, and disciplining the militia for use in the states. Obviously, the question of whether continued surveillance over the operations of the National Guard should be maintained has been committed under the Constitution to the political branches directly responsible to the elective process. Courts have no competence to evaluate professional decisions concerning the composition, training, equipping, and control of a military force. The Court observed, however, that its decision did not mean that conduct of the National Guard is always beyond judicial review whether by way of damages or injunctive relief.

Colgrove v. Battin, 413 U.S. 149 (1973)

Facts: A federal district court established a local rule providing for a jury of six in the trial of civil cases. That local rule was challenged as unconstitutional under the Seventh Amendment which allegedly required 12-member juries and invalid under the Federal Rules of Civil Procedure (FRCP) because inconsistent therewith. (Rule 83 of the FRCP allows district courts to make local rules not inconsistent with the FRCP.)

Question: Is the local rule providing for six-man jury trials in civil cases unconstitutional under the Seventh Amendment or invalid under the FRCP?

Decision: No. Opinion by Justice Brennan. Vote: 5-4.

Reasons: The Seventh Amendment provides that "[i]n suits at common law . . . the right of trial by jury shall be preserved. . . . On its face, this language is not directed to jury characteristics, such as size, but rather defines the kind of cases for which jury trial is preserved. . . ." After reviewing the history of the Seventh Amendment, the Court concluded that it preserved the substance of the common-law characteristics of trial by jury, as distinguished from mere matters of form or procedure. Noting that there has been no discernible difference between results reached by 12- or six-member juries, the Court concluded that a jury of six satisfies the Seventh Amendment's guarantee of trial by jury in civil cases.

The Court also rejected the contention that Rule 48 of the FRCP, which authorizes parties to stipulate that a civil jury consist of less than 12 jurors, by negative implication forbade local rules mandating juries of less than 12. The Court concluded that Rule 48 deals only with party stipulations and was not intended to foreclose local rules concerning jury size.

NAACP v. New York, 413 U.S. 345 (1973)

Facts: A lower federal court denied a motion by the National Association for the Advancement of Colored People (NAACP) to intervene as a party defendant in a suit initially brought by New York against the United States to remove three New York counties from the coverage of the Voting Rights Act Amendments of 1970 (Act). (A county within the coverage of the Act cannot change or add voting requirements except upon proof that such changes or additions will have neither the purpose nor effect of abridging the right to vote on account of race or color. A county may be removed from the Act's coverage upon proof that for the previous 10 years no test or device had been used to deprive persons of the right to vote on account of race or color.) The defendant United States had virtually conceded that the three New York counties should be removed from the Act's coverage, and the NAACP sought intervention to produce evidence showing that voting tests or devices had in fact been used discriminatorily during the previous 10 years.

Question: Did the trial judge abuse his discretion in denying the motion of the NAACP to intervene under Rule 24 of the Federal Rules of Civil Procedure?

Decision: No. Opinion by Justice Blackmun. Vote: 6-2.

Reasons: Rule 24 requires that a motion to intervene be timely. In this case, the following four factors tend to show that the motion was untimely and that the denial was not an abuse of the trial court's discretion: (1) the NAACP had notice of the suit long before their motion to intervene, (2) the suit was almost concluded when the motion was made, (3) there were no unusual circumstances warranting intervention, and (4) with primary elections rapidly approaching in New York, granting intervention possessed the potential for seriously disrupting the state's electoral process.

Hall v. Cole, 412 U.S. 1 (1973)

Facts: A former union member, expelled from his union for introducing resolutions at a union meeting which protested actions by certain union officers, sued the union under section 102 of the Labor-Management Reporting and Disclosure Act (LMRDA) claiming that his expulsion violated his right of free speech as secured by section 101(a) of the LMRDA. A lower federal court ordered the former union member permanently reinstated and awarded him $5,500 in counsel fees against the union.

Question: Was the lower federal court's award of counsel fees proper?

Decision: Yes. Opinion by Justice Brennan. Vote: 6-2.

Reasons: "Although the traditional American rule ordinarily disfavors the allowance of attorneys' fees in the absence of statutory or contractual authorization, federal courts, in the exercise of their equitable powers, may award attorneys' fees when the interests of justice so require." A federal court may award attorneys' fees to a successful party (1) whose opponent has litigated in bad faith, or (2) whose successful litigation confers "a substantial benefit on members of an ascertainable class, and where the court's jurisdiction over the subject matter of the suit makes possible an award that will operate to spread the costs proportionately among them." This case falls within the latter situation because the successful litigant rendered a substantial service to his union and all union members by dispelling any chill earlier cast upon the free speech rights of any and all union members. Moreover, nothing in the LMRDA indicates that Congress intended to preclude federal courts from using their equitable power to award counsel fees in these circumstances. Finding that the lower federal court did not abuse its discretion in awarding counsel fees, the Court concluded that the award was proper.

Palmore v. United States, 411 U.S. 389 (1973)

Facts: Charged with a felony under the District of Columbia Code and subject to trial before one of the District of Columbia judges appointed by the President for a 15-year term, the defendant moved to dismiss his indictment on the ground that he was constitutionally entitled to be tried before a court ordained and established in accordance with Article III of the United States Constitution. Article III, Section 1 states that all judges sitting on courts established pursuant to that section (which courts are limited to hearing cases within the federal judicial power as set forth in Article III, Section 2) shall hold their offices for life during good behavior and receive compensation which shall not be diminished during their continuance in office. The criminal statute under which the defendant was charged and the statute creating the District of Columbia court before which he was to be tried were passed by Congress pursuant to its plenary power to legislate for the District of Columbia under Article I, Section 8, clause 17 of the Constitution.

Question: Are defendants charged with violating District of Columbia statutes constitutionally entitled to be tried by a court ordained and established in accordance with Article III, Section 1 of the Constitution?

Decision: No. Opinion by Justice White. Vote: 8-1.

Reasons: The defendant's claim was that because the criminal statute under which he was charged was passed by Congress and thus was a case potentially falling within the "judicial power" of the United States under Article III, Section 2 (which extends such power to cases arising under federal statutes) an Article III judge was constitutionally required to preside over his trial. In other words, the defendant asserted that criminal offenses under the laws passed by Congress may not be prosecuted except in courts established pursuant to Article III. This contention must be rejected because Congress is not constitutionally compelled to create lower federal courts to try federal criminal cases and Congress may leave such cases to state courts and state court judges who do not enjoy the protections prescribed for federal judges in Article III of life tenure at undiminished compensation. "[B]oth Congress and this Court have recognized that state courts are appropriate forums in which federal questions and federal crimes may at times be tried; and that the requirements of Art. III, which are applicable where laws of national applicability and affairs of national concern are at stake, must in proper circumstances give way to accommodate plenary grants of power to Congress to legislate with respect to specialized areas having particularized needs and warranting distinctive treatment. . . . We do not discount the importance attached to the tenure and salary provisions of Art. III, but we conclude that Congress was not required to provide an Art. III court for the trial of criminal cases arising under its laws applicable only within the District of Columbia." The defendant's trial in the District of Columbia court was authorized by Congress's Article I power to legislate for the District of Columbia in all cases whatsoever. The defendant "was no more disadvantaged and no more entitled to an Art. III judge than any other citizen of any of the 50 states who is tried for a strictly local crime. Nor did his trial by a nontenured judge deprive him of due process of law under the Fifth Amendment any more than the trial of the citizens of the various States for local crimes by judges without protection as to tenure deprive them of due process of law under the Fourteenth Amendment."

Goosby v. *Osser*, 409 U.S. 512 (1973)

Facts: Prisoners awaiting trial and confined in Philadelphia County prisons either because unable to afford bail or because charged with nonbailable offenses challenged the constitutionality of the Pennsylvania Election Code on the ground that the code absolutely denied them the right to vote in violation of equal protection and due process. The complaint alleged that the prisoners were prohibited from voting by absentee ballot, prohibited from leaving prison to register or vote, and not provided prison facilities to register or vote. Since the prisoners sought to enjoin the enforcement of a state statute, they requested a three-judge federal court to hear their case in accord with 28 U.S. Code, 2281 which provides that three-judge courts shall hear all suits seeking a ". . . permanent injunction restraining the enforcement . . . of any State statute . . . upon the ground of the unconstitutionality of such statute. . . ." A lower federal court refused to call a three-judge court and dismissed the complaint.

Question: Should a three-judge court have been called under 28 U.S. Code, 2281 to hear the prisoners' suit challenging the constitutionality of certain provisions of the Pennsylvania Election Code and seeking to enjoin their enforcement?

Decision: Yes. Opinion by Justice Brennan. Vote: 9-0.

Reasons: Section 2281 "does not require the convening of a 3-judge court when the constitutional attack upon the state statutes is insubstantial. . . . A claim is insubstantial only if its unsoundness so clearly results from the previous decisions of this Court so as to foreclose the subject and leave no room for the inference that the question sought to be raised can be the subject of controversy." The Court rejected the argument that its decision in *McDonald* v. *Board of Election Commissioners,* 394 U.S. 802 (1969), rendered the prisoners' claims insubstantial. In *McDonald* the Court rejected a claim that pre-trial detainees, who were registered to vote but denied the use of absentee ballots, were denied equal protection because of the absence of any allegation by the detainees that other means to exercise their franchise were not provided. In this case, however, the prisoners alleged that absolutely no means to exercise their franchise were provided, and thus *McDonald* did not foreclose their constitutional claim attacking the Pennsylvania Election Code.

United States v. Little Lake Misere Land Co., 412 U.S. 580 (1973)

Facts: A Louisiana statute retroactively abrogated the terms of a written agreement between the United States and certain private persons which provided that mineral rights on certain lands acquired by the United States would be reserved to the sellers for 10 years before vesting in the United States. The statute applied only to lands acquired by the United States and operated so as to retroactively divest the United States of the mineral rights it had acquired pursuant to written agreement. The United States refused to give up its mineral rights contending that the Louisiana statute was inapplicable to its land transactions providing for the transfer of certain mineral rights.

Question: Was the Louisiana statute constitutionally inapplicable to the land transaction between the United States and private persons?

Decision: Yes. Opinion by Chief Jusice Burger. Vote: 8-0.

Reasons: The right of the United States to seek legal redress for duly authorized proprietary transactions is a federal right and federal law governs the legal consequences of such transactions. And if Congress has not provided the governing law, then it is for the federal courts to fashion the governing rule according to its own standards. Thus, the land acquisition agreement in question should seemingly be governed by federal law. However, it is unnecessary to decide this question because in no event could the Louisiana statute be applicable because its retroactive abrogation of contract terms entered into by the United States would impair the ability of the United States to buy and sell land as contemplated by the Migratory Bird Conservation Act. The Louisiana statute being inapplicable to the land transaction in question, the Court determined that under either federal law or some residual state law the United States was entitled to the disputed mineral rights.

Federal Statutes

The Court decided important cases this term involving federal statutes in the fields of administrative law, antitrust, civil rights, consumer credit, environmental law, federal tort claims, food and drug law, labor law, patents, securities regulation, taxation, and welfare.

Administrative Law. The Court decided two important cases in this field concerning standing and the Freedom of Information Act. In one case, the Court upheld the standing of an environmental group under the Administrative Procedure Act to challenge the legality of freight rate increases on recyclable materials. That group contended that an environmental impact statement was required before any increase was put into effect regarding recyclable materials and that increased freight rates on these materials would ultimately harm the environment. In the other case the Court interpreted the Freedom of Information Act to give the government absolute power to withhold from disclosure any classified document. Concerning the exemption from disclosure for inter-agency and intra-agency memoranda, however, the Court concluded that all factual data embedded in those memoranda must be disclosed although policy statements and opinions could be withheld from public scrutiny.

United States v. *Students Challenging Regulatory Agency Procedures*, 412 U.S. 669 (1973)

Facts: Under the Interstate Commerce Act, a railroad seeking a rate increase must provide at least 30 days' notice to the Interstate Commerce Commission (ICC) and the public before putting the rate into effect. During that 30-day period, the ICC may suspend the operation of the proposed rate for a maximum of seven months pending an investigation and decision on the lawfulness of the new rates. Proceeding under this statutory scheme, almost all railroads filed notice of a 2.5 percent surcharge on nearly all freight rates. The ICC refused to suspend this surcharge while investigating its lawfulness. (Under the Interstate Commerce Act, shippers can recover payments for charges later determined to have been illegal.) Environmental groups, including Students Challenging Regulatory Agency Procedures (SCRAP), challenged the legality of the surcharge in federal district court alleging that failure to suspend the surcharge would cause their members environmental harm. SCRAP alleged that the challenged rate structure would discourage the use of "recyclable" materials and promote the use of new raw materials, thereby adversely affecting the environment by encouraging unwarranted mining, lumbering, and other extractive activities. The district court entered an injunction forbidding the collection of the 2.5 percent surcharge on the ground that the ICC had failed to file a proper environmental impact statement concerning the effects of the challenged surcharge under the National Environmental Policy Act of 1969 (NEPA).

Questions: Did SCRAP have standing to challenge the legality of the proposed surcharge? Was the district court injunction forbidding the implementation of the surcharge proper?

Decision: Yes to the first question and no to the second. Opinion by Justice Stewart. Vote: 5-3 on the first question and 6-2 on the second.

Reasons: A group has standing to challenge governmental agency action under the Administrative Procedure Act if the challenged action would cause it injury in fact (economic, aesthetic, or otherwise) and is allegedly in violation of a statute arguably intended to protect that group. SCRAP, on the basis of its allegations, met the twofold requirement for standing. NEPA was intended to protect environmental groups like SCRAP, and SCRAP had alleged that the challenged surcharge would in fact cause its members aesthetic injury. The Court noted, however, that SCRAP must be able to prove its allegations of injury caused by the challenged surcharge in order to maintain the lawsuit.

The district court injunction prohibiting the 2.5 percent surcharge from taking effect was overturned under the authority of *Arrow Transportation Co.* v. *Southern R. Co.,* 372 U.S. 658 (1963), which held that, under the Interstate Commerce Act, Congress had vested exclusive power in the ICC to suspend rates pending its final decision on their lawfulness and had deliberately extinguished judicial power to grant such relief. Because the ICC had not finally determined the lawfulness of the proposed surcharge, the district court lacked power to issue the injunction.

Environmental Protection Agency v. *Mink,* 410 U.S. 73 (1973)

Facts: Congresswoman Patsy Mink and 32 of her House colleagues sued the Environmental Protection Agency (EPA) under the Freedom of Information Act (FIA), 5 U.S. Code, 552(a)(3), to compel the disclosure of nine documents prepared by the Undersecretaries' Committee of the National Security Council established to advise President Nixon on the safety of the underground nuclear test known as "Cannikan," which took place on Amchitka Island, Alaska. Eight of the documents had been classified top secret and secret pursuant to Executive Order 10501. EPA defended on grounds that the nine documents were exempted from the general disclosure requirements of section 552(a)(3) by virtue of sections 552(b)(1) and (b)(5), which protect from disclosure "matters . . . specifically required by Executive order to be kept secret in the interest of national defense or foreign policy" and "inter-agency or intra-agency memorandums or letters which would not be available by law to a party . . . in litigation with the agency." A lower federal court ruled that all top secret and secret documents alleged to fall within the section 552(b)(1) exemption (national defense exemption) should be submitted to the court for *in camera* inspection to sift out and disclose their nonsecret portions; all documents alleged to fall within the section 552(b)(5) exemption (inter-agency memorandum exemption) were ordered to be inspected *in camera* to determine if factual data therein could be separated and disclosed without impinging on the policy-making and decisional processes intended to be protected by this exemption.

Questions: Did the lower federal court err in requiring documents admittedly falling within the national defense exemption from disclosure under the FIA to be inspected *in camera* in order to sift out and disclose any nonsecret portions? Did the lower federal court err in mandating that all documents admittedly falling within the inter-agency memorandum exemption be inspected *in camera* and that all factual information therein unrelated to decisional processes be disclosed?

Decision: Yes to both questions. Opinion by Justice White. Vote: 5-3.

Reasons: After tracing the legislative history of the national defense exemption, the Court concluded that Congress intended that any document that had been classified pursuant to executive order was to be exempt from disclosure *in toto* under that exemption and courts were given no authority to sift out and disclose nonsecret portions of the documents. The Court made clear, however, that Congress could change this result by amending the national defense exemption.

The inter-agency memorandum exemption, the Court concluded, protected only matters so intertwined with policy making that their disclosure would impinge frank communications between policy makers and agencies. Thus, the Court held it was proper for the lower court to compel the disclosure of all factual data in the documents falling within the inter-agency exemption that would not compromise "the private remainder of the documents." However, the Court stated that the government should be given an opportunity, by affidavit or otherwise, to show that *in camera* inspection of such documents was unnecessary to ensure that factual information was not being illegally withheld.

United States v. Florida East Coast Railway Co., 410 U.S. 224 (1973)

Facts: Two railroad companies sued to set aside the incentive per diem rates for the use of railroad freight cars established by the Interstate Commerce Commission (ICC) to encourage the purchase of freight cars and thereby to alleviate a nationwide shortage. The railroads based their suit on the ground that the ICC failed to hold a proper hearing before setting the rates as required by sections 556 and 557 of the Administrative Procedure Act (APA) and section 1(14)(a) of the Interstate Commerce Act (ICA). The ICC promulgated the rates after giving notice to the railroads and an opportunity to submit written data and views in accordance with section 553 of the APA. The railroads argued that they were entitled to a more extensive hearing with rights of oral argument and cross-examination under sections 556 and 557 of the APA by virtue of section 553(c), which requires such hearings "[w]hen rules are required by statute to be made on the record after opportunity for an agency hearing." Section 1(14)(a) of the ICA requires the ICC to hold a "hearing" before setting rates, and the railroads contended that this section of the ICA was a statute requiring the per diem freight car rates to be made "on the record after opportunity for an agency hearing" within the meaning of section 553(c) of the APA.

Question: Did the ICC violate either the APA or section 1(14)(a) of the ICA by failing to provide a more extensive hearing before setting per diem freight car rates?

Decision: No. Opinion by Justice Rehnquist. Vote: 6-2.

Reasons: In *United States* v. *Allegheny-Ludlum Steel Corp.,* 406 U.S. 742 (1972), the Court held that section 1(14)(a) of the ICA authorizing the ICC to act "after hearing" did not require a rule to be made "on the record" within the meaning of section 553(c) of the APA. That decision compels the conclusion that the ICC did not violate the APA when it failed to hold extensive hearings before setting per diem freight car rates. Reasoning by analogy from the requirements of notice and an opportunity to present written views before rules are established under section 553 of the APA, the Court stated that the term "hearing" as used in section 1(14)(a) of the ICA did not "embrace either the right to present evidence orally and to cross-examine opposing witnesses, or the right to present oral argument to the agency's decisionmaker." Thus, the Court held that the ICA was not violated by the limited hearing procedures used by the ICC before setting the challenged freight car rates.

Atchison, Topeka & Santa Fe Railway Co. v. Wichita Board of Trade, 412 U.S. 800 (1973)

Facts: The Interstate Commerce Commission (ICC) concluded after a hearing that railroads should be permitted to charge shippers separately for in-transit inspection of grain, reasoning that the proposed charges were not excessive in amount and were needed to reduce the number of in-transit inspections which resulted in a substantial decrease in the number of freight cars available for use. (In-transit inspections had formerly been performed free of charge.) Shippers successfully challenged the ICC order in lower federal court on the ground that the ICC had not adequately justified its failure to follow its well-established rule that separate charges for accessorial services previously performed as part of long-haul rates would not be permitted without substantial evidence that both the additional charge and the long-haul rates were reasonable. The lower federal court remanded the case to the ICC for further findings along these lines and enjoined the proposed charges from becoming effective until ordered by the court.

Questions: Did the ICC inadequately explain its reasons for permitting the proposed in-transit grain inspection charge? Did the lower federal court properly enjoin the proposed charges from taking effect?

Decision: Yes to the first question and no to the second. Opinion by Justice Marshall. Vote: 5-3.

Reasons: *SEC* v. *Chenery Corp.,* 332 U.S. 194 (1947) established the fundamental rule of administrative law that an agency must set forth clearly the grounds on which it acted before a court will review its orders. In this case, the ICC failed to determine whether the long-haul rates no longer including in-transit grain inspections would still be reasonable, a departure from its prior practices. No explanation was given as to why the ICC did not require the railroads to establish the reasonableness of the long-haul rates by substantial evidence. Thus, the lower federal court properly remanded the case to the ICC for further findings or reasons explaining its order.

The Court nevertheless concluded that the injunction suspending the implementation of the proposed charges made by the railroads was improper. Under 49 U.S. Code, 6(3) and 15(1), carriers may put into effect any rate that the ICC has not declared unreasonable. In *Arrow Transportation Co.* v. *Southern R. Co.,* 372 U.S. 658 (1963), the Court held generally that only the ICC can suspend proposed rates from taking effect. Although in some circumstances a court's equity power to maintain the status quo or prevent irreparable injury following a remand might justify enjoining rates from taking effect, no such circumstances existed in this case because procedures are available for shippers to recover any excess charges.

Camp v. Pitts, 411 U.S. 138 (1973)

Facts: The comptroller of the currency denied an application for a certificate authorizing the organization of a new bank in Hartsville, South Carolina, under 12 U.S. Code, 27 on the ground that a bank was not needed in that area. As permitted by federal law and federal regulations, the comptroller rendered his decision without holding a hearing. In reviewing the validity of the denial on the ground that the comptroller inadequately explained his decision, a federal court of appeals ruled that a federal district court should hold a trial *de novo* on the factual reasons relied upon to justify the denial and to reverse the comptroller's decision if the bank applicants proved by a preponderance of the evidence that it was "capricious or an abuse of discretion."

Question: Were the trial procedures outlined by the court of appeals for the remand in this case to the district court erroneous?

Decision: Yes. Per curiam opinion. Vote: 9-0.

Reasons: In *Citizens to Preserve Overton Park* v. *Volpe,* 401 U.S. 402 (1971), the Court held that a challenged administrative decision should be subject to *de novo* judicial review under 5 U.S. Code, 706(2)(F) "only where there are inadequate factfinding procedures in an adjudicatory hearing or where judicial proceedings are brought to enforce certain administrative action." (Section 706 (2)(F) provides that a reviewing court may set aside administrative action "unwarranted by the facts to the extent that the facts are subject to a trial de novo ....") Neither of the situations justifying *de novo* review under section 706(2)(F) is applicable in this case because the comptroller's decision is challenged solely on the ground that it lacked adequate explanation. Thus, the comptroller's decision was properly subject to judicial review under 5 U.S. Code, 706(2)(A) which provides for invalidating administrative action found to be arbitrary, capricious, or an abuse of discretion. "In applying that standard, the focal point for judicial review should be the administrative record already in existence, not some new record made initially in the reviewing court." The Court concluded that if the comptroller's finding that a new bank in Hartsville, South Carolina would be an uneconomic venture in light of the available banking needs and banking services was "not sustainable on the administrative record made, then the Comptroller's decision must be vacated and the matter remanded to him for further consideration." However, the Court held it was error for the federal court of appeals to order a trial *de novo* to test the validity of the comptroller's ruling.

Butz v. Glover Livestock Commission Co., 411 U.S. 183 (1973)

Facts: A stockyard operator, authorized to sell consigned livestock on commission under the Packers and Stockyards Act (Act), was found by the secretary of agriculture to have willfully violated, *inter alia,* sections 307(a) and 312(a) of the Act by "intentionally weigh[ing] . . . livestock at less than their true weights, issue[ing] scale tickets and accountings to . . . consignors on the basis of . . . false weights, and pay[ing] . . . consignors on the basis of . . . false weights." The secretary thus ordered the livestock operator to cease and desist from the violations and suspended the operator from market trading in livestock for 20 days. On judicial review under the Administrative Procedure Act, a court of appeals set aside the secretary's suspension order because: (1) the secretary had not suspended stockyard operators for similar violations in other cases, and (2) the cease-and-desist order coupled with the damaging publicity surrounding the proceedings was a sufficient penalty to deter the practices which the secretary was seeking to eliminate.

Question: Did the court of appeals err in setting aside the secretary's 20-day suspension order under the Administrative Procedure Act?

Decision: Yes. Opinion by Justice Brennan. Vote: 7-2.

Reasons: "[W]here Congress has entrusted an administrative agency with the responsibility of selecting the means of achieving the statutory policy 'the relation of remedy to policy is peculiarly a matter for administrative competence.'" Under the Administrative Procedure Act, the court of appeals should not have overturned the secretary's 20-day suspension order for violation of the Packers and Stockyards Act unless it was "unwarranted in law or . . . without justification in fact. . . ." The fact that the secretary may not have uniformly imposed suspension as a sanction for similar violations of the Act did not render his order "unwarranted in law" because the secretary has broad discretion to impose the sanctions he deems necessary to deter violations and to achieve the objectives of that statute. Neither was the suspension "without justification in fact" because the record showed the stockyard operator had previously disregarded warnings from the department of agriculture that he was improperly underweighing consigned livestock. Thus, the Court held that the overturning by the court of appeals "of the suspension authorized by the statute was an impermissible intrusion into the administrative domain."

Antitrust. Of the Court's seven antitrust decisions this term, the most notable concerned a lower court judgment of some $145 million against Hughes Tool Co. in favor of Trans World Airlines. Justice Douglas, writing for a 6-2 majority, set aside the judgment on the ground that the Civil Aeronautics Board had given Hughes Tool antitrust immunity which covered the challenged activities. In other similar antitrust suits concerning the merger of shipping companies and the distribution of electric power, the Court held that no immunity was conferred on the respective defendants in those cases by virtue of the Shipping Act of 1916 or the Federal Power Act.

The Court strengthened the hand of the government in antitrust enforcement by holding that the Federal Power Commission must consider anticompetitive effects before authorizing a public utility to issue bonds and by concluding that the United States could challenge the validity of patents in antitrust suits even though those patents had not been used to support anticompetitive conduct.

In a case partially reflecting a tendency by the Court to uphold the government's position in nearly all antitrust suits, the Court broadened the power of the United States to prevent anticompetitive mergers under section 7 of the Clayton Act in ruling that a lower federal court erred in failing to consider the procompetitive influence of an outside brewer on a regional market (as a potential entrant) before permitting it to merge with a brewer already in that market.

Hughes Tool Co. v. Trans World Airlines, Inc., 409 U.S. 363 (1973)

Facts: A default judgment was entered for over $145 million in favor of Trans World Airlines (TWA) against Hughes Tool Company (Toolco) on the ground that Toolco violated the antitrust laws while in control of TWA by using its control to delay the delivery of 63 jet aircraft to TWA, an action which resulted in competitive disadvantage to TWA. During the years in question, Toolco owned over 40 percent of the outstanding TWA stock and itself manufactured commercial aircraft. Toolco unsuccessfully contended that the challenged transactions had been approved by the Civil Aeronautics Board (CAB) pursuant to sections 408 and 414 of the Federal Aviation Act (Act) and thus were immune from attack under the antitrust laws.

Question: Did CAB approval of Toolco's control over and relations with TWA under sections 408 and 414 of the Act immunize the challenged transactions involving the sale of commercial jet aircraft from attack under the antitrust laws?

Decision: Yes. Opinion by Justice Douglas. Vote: 6-2.

Reasons: Under section 408 of the Act the CAB was required, in approving Toolco's control of TWA, to consider whether Toolco's control of TWA would promote monopoly or adversely affect competition in the air transportation field. Moreover, section 414 of the Act immunizes from antitrust liability any conduct approved, authorized, or required by any CAB order issued under section 408. Noting that "every acquisition or lease of aircraft by TWA from Toolco and each financing of TWA by Toolco" from 1944 to 1960 received CAB approval under section 408 and that the CAB had found Toolco's stewardship of TWA to be in the public interest, the Court concluded that Toolco's conduct in delaying the delivery of 63 jet aircraft to TWA had received immunity from antitrust challenge by virtue of the CAB's oversight.

While reaffirming its view that the Federal Aviation Act does not completely displace the antitrust laws, the Court maintained that when "the CAB authorizes control of an air carrier to be acquired by another person or corporation and where it specifically authorizes as in the public interest specific transactions between the parent and the subsidiary, the way in which that control is exercised in those precise situations is under the surveillance of the CAB, not in the hands of those who can invoke the sanctions of antitrust laws."

Federal Maritime Commission v. Seatrain Lines, Inc., 411 U.S. 726 (1973)

Facts: Section 15 of the Shipping Act of 1916 requires all persons subject to that Act to file with the Federal Maritime Commission (Commission) every agreement within specified categories reached with any other person subject to the Act. Under section 15, the Commission is empowered to disapprove, cancel, or modify any such agreement which it deems unjustly discriminatory, detrimental to the commerce of the United States, contrary to the public interest, or violative of the terms of the Act. The Commission is also directed to approve all other such agreements, and approval exempts such agreements from the antitrust laws. Pursuant to section 15, the Commission attempted to assert its regulatory jurisdiction over an agreement by one shipping company (Oceanic) to sell all its assets to another shipping company (Pacific). Oceanic and Pacific contended that the agreement for the sale of assets which created no ongoing obligations between the two did not fall within the Commission's purview under section 15.

Question: Does a contract calling for the acquisition of one shipping carrier by another carrier, creating no ongoing obligations between the two, constitute an agreement within the Commission's purview under section 15 of the Shipping Act of 1916?

Decision: No. Opinion by Justice Marshall. Vote: 9-0.

Reasons: Although section 15 does not clearly embrace or exclude discrete merger or acquisition-of-assets agreements, when read in light of the rest of the statutory scheme embodied in the shipping act, it would make no sense if "read to encompass one-time agreements creating no continuing obligations." Under the shipping act the Commission regulates agreements between carriers: (1) fixing rates or fares, (2) pooling or apportioning earnings, losses, or traffic, (3) allotting ports, (4) regulating freight or passenger traffic, and (5) providing any type of cooperative working arrangement. Section 15 thus "envisions a continuing supervisory role for the Commission," which cannot be applied to one-time sale-of-assets agreements providing for no continuing obligation needing supervision. The statutory pattern of the shipping act, together with its legislative history and the established rule that statutes exempting agreements from the antitrust laws should be strictly construed, compels the conclusion that section 15 was not intended to confer jurisdiction on the Commission to regulate and approve merger and acquisition-of-assets agreements thereby exempting them from the antitrust laws.

Otter Tail Power Company v. United States, 410 U.S. 366 (1973)

Facts: In a civil antitrust suit brought by the United States against Otter Tail Power Company (Otter Tail), a private electric utility company, the district court found that Otter Tail had monopolized the retail distribution of electric power in its 510-town service area and thus had violated section 2 of the Sherman Act. The district court ruled that Otter Tail violated section 2 by attempting to prevent communities in which its retail distribution franchises had expired (the franchises were limited from 10 to 20 years) from replacing it with a municipal distribution system by using the following principal means: (1) refusing to sell power at wholesale to proposed municipal systems in the communities where it had been retailing power, (2) refusing to "wheel" power to such systems (that is, to transfer by direct transmission or displacement electric power from one utility to another over the facilities of an intermediate utility), (3) instituting and supporting litigation designed to prevent or delay establishment of municipal systems, and (4) invoking provisions in its transmission contracts with several other power suppliers for the purpose of denying the municipal systems access to other suppliers by use of Otter Tail's transmission systems. The district court's remedial decree enjoined Otter Tail from: (1) refusing to sell electric power at wholesale to existing or proposed municipal electric power systems in the areas it served, (2) refusing to wheel electric power generated by Otter Tail over the lines of other electric power systems to existing or proposed municipal systems in the area, (3) entering into or enforcing any contract prohibiting use of Otter Tail's lines to wheel electric power to municipal electric power systems or limiting the customers or areas to which Otter Tail or any other electric power company might sell electric power, and (4) engaging in litigation against municipalities and their officials which had voted to establish municipal electric power systems for the purpose of delaying, preventing or interfering with the establishment of a municipal electric power system.

Question: Was the district court's finding of a section 2 violation of the Sherman Act and remedial decree proper?

Decision: All the findings and the remedial decree were proper, except for the injunction against Otter Tail's engaging in future litigation against municipalities. Opinion by Justice Douglas. Vote: 4-3.

Reasons: The antitrust charge against Otter Tail focused on the methods used to prevent the towns it served from establishing their own municipal electric systems when Otter Tail's franchises expired. In this connection, the record adequately supported the lower court's findings that Otter Tail refused to sell energy at wholesale to new municipal electrical distribution systems, refused to wheel power, and instituted litigation challenging the legality of municipal revenue bonds issued to finance the building of municipal distribution systems. This litigation had the effect of appreciably slowing efforts to establish municipal systems and was instituted with the expectation of foreclosing or destroying competition in the retail distribution of electricity in the areas Otter Tail served. Otter Tail clearly had a monopoly over the retail distribution of energy in the relevant geographic market because it served 465 of 510 towns therein. The use of its monopoly power in the aforementioned ways to destroy threatened competition violated section 2 of the Sherman Act under Supreme Court decisions in *Lorain Journal* v. *United States*, 342 U.S. 143 (1951) and *Eastman Kodak Co.* v. *Southern Photo Materials Co.*, 273 U.S. 359 (1927).

The Court rejected the contention that Otter Tail's refusals to wholesale or wheel power to its municipal customers were immune from antitrust attack by reason of section 202(b) of the Federal Power Act, which gives the Federal Power Commission (Commission) authority to compel involuntary interconnections of power. Noting that repeal of an antitrust law by implication from a regulatory statute is a strongly disfavored conclusion and that the Commission's determination of whether interconnections should be ordered did not emphasize antitrust considerations, the Court concluded that the Commission's limited authority "to order interconnections was not intended to be a substitute for or immunize Otter Tail from antitrust regulation for refusing to deal with municipal corporations."

The lower court's injunction forbidding Otter Tail from engaging in litigation having the purpose of delaying the establishment of municipal electric systems was issued under an erroneous view of the law in the belief that such litigation could not be immune from antitrust challenge. In *Eastern Railroad Conference* v. *Noerr Motor Freight, Inc.*, 365 U.S. 127 (1961), and *California Motor Transport Co.* v. *Trucking Unlimited*, 404 U.S. 508 (1972), the Court held that legitimate attempts to influence the legislative, executive, and judicial branches of government were immune from antitrust challenge, but that if such attempts were a "mere sham" to interfere with the business of an actual or potential competitor then the immunity would fall. The Court thus remanded the case to the district court to determine whether Otter Tail's litigation came within the "mere sham" exception to antitrust immunity and thus could properly be enjoined.

Ricci v. *Chicago Mercantile Exchange*, 409 U.S. 289 (1973)

Facts: Ricci sued the Chicago Mercantile Exchange (Exchange), two Exchange officers, an Exchange director and member, alleging that they unlawfully transferred his Exchange membership pursuant to a conspiracy to restrain trade in violation of the Sherman Act. Because the challenged conduct arguably violated some provisions of the Commodity Exchange Act which were enforced by the Commodity Exchange Commission (Commission), composed of the secretaries of agriculture and commerce and the attorney general, a lower federal court ruled that the court suit should be stayed until the Commission determined whether the conduct violated any provisions of the Commodity Exchange Act.

Question: Did the lower federal court err in staying the court proceedings until the Commission ruled on the legality of the challenged conduct under the Commodity Exchange Act?

Decisions: No. Opinion by Justice White. Vote: 5-4.

Reasons: "[W]hen conduct seemingly within the reach of the antitrust laws is also at least arguably protected or prohibited by another regulatory statute enacted by Congress," such conduct is immune from antitrust scrutiny "only if necessary" to make the regulatory scheme work and "even then only to the minimum extent necessary." The Court concluded that, in this case, the antitrust suit should be stayed until the Commission examined the Ricci-Exchange dispute in light of the regulatory scheme of the Commodity Exchange Act because: (1) "it will be essential for the Antitrust Court to determine whether the Commodity Exchange Act or any of its provisions are 'incompatible with the maintenance of the antitrust action' . . .; (2) . . . some facets of the dispute between Ricci and the Exchange are within the statutory jurisdiction of the Commodity Exchange Commission; and (3) . . . adjudication of that dispute by the Commission promises to be of material aid in resolving the [antitrust] immunity question."

United States v. *Falstaff Brewing Corporation,* 410 U.S. 526 (1973)

Facts: In 1965 after Falstaff Brewing Corporation (Falstaff), a regional brewer not selling in the New England market, acquired the Narragansett Brewing Company (Narragansett), a local brewer with 20 percent of the New England market, the United States sought to undo the acquisition under section 7 of the Clayton Act, which prohibits mergers whose effect "may be substantially to lessen competition, or tend to create a monopoly." The United States alleged that the acquisition would violate section 7 by substantially lessening competition in the production and sale of beer in the New England market because: (1) Falstaff was a potential entrant, and (2) the acquisition eliminated competition that would have existed had Falstaff entered the market *de novo* or by acquiring and expanding a smaller firm, making a so-called toe-hold acquisition. At the time of its acquisition of Narragansett in 1965, Falstaff controlled 5.9 percent of the national beer market; Narragansett was the largest New England brewer with 20 percent of the market; the number of brewers operating plants in New England had decreased from 11 to 6 in the past eight years; and the eight largest sellers of beer in New England controlled 81.2 percent of the market. After a trial on the merits, the district court dismissed the complaint, finding that Falstaff would not have entered the New England beer market *de novo;* that competition in that market had not diminished subsequent to the challenged acquisition of Narragansett; and that the government failed to establish that the acquisition would result in a substantial lessening of competition.

Question: Did the district court err in ruling that the acquisition did not violate section 7 of the Clayton Act solely because it found that Falstaff, as a matter of fact, would never have entered the New England beer market *de novo* without considering other pro-competitive influences exerted by Falstaff from its position on the fringe of the market?

Decision: Yes. Opinion by Justice White. Vote: 7-2.

Reasons: "Section 7 of the Clayton Act forbids mergers in any line of commerce where the effect may be substantially to lessen competition or tend to create a monopoly." Section 7 forbids acquisitions by a company "not competing in the market but so situated as to be a potential competitor and likely to exercise substantial influence on market behavior." Although the district court concluded that Falstaff would not have entered the New England beer market *de novo,* it failed to consider whether Falstaff was a potential competitor in this market in the sense that its position on the edge of the market was a pro-competitive influence. If Falstaff was so positioned, its acquisition of Narragansett might well violate section 7. The Court thus remanded the case to the district court for a proper appraisal of the "economic facts about Falstaff and the New England market in order to determine whether in any realistic sense Falstaff could be said to be a potential competitor on the fringe of the market with likely influence on existing competition."

United States v. Glaxo Group Limited, 410 U.S. 52 (1973)

Facts: Imperial Chemical Industries Limited (ICI) and Glaxo Group Limited (Glaxo), British drug companies engaged in the manufacture and sale of the drug griseofulvin, were found to have violated the Sherman Act by restricting the sale and resale of the bulk form of the drug in various agreements among themselves and with licensees. ICI owned various patents on the dosage form of the drug and Glaxo owned patents on a method for manufacturing the drug in bulk form and in dosage form. ICI and Glaxo granted various United States companies licenses under their bulk and dosage-form licenses but restricted the licensees from selling the drug in bulk form. To remedy the antitrust violations committed by ICI and Glaxo, the government requested the lower federal court to order mandatory, nondiscriminatory sales of the bulk form of the drug plus reasonable-royalty licensing of the ICI and Glaxo patents, and to declare one of Glaxo's patents invalid even though Glaxo did not rely on this patent as a defense to the antitrust suit. The lower federal court refused the government's request and limited its remedy to enjoining ICI and Glaxo from employing bulk-sale restrictions.

Questions: Can the United States challenge the validity of a patent when prosecuting an antitrust action if the patent is not relied on as a defense? Did the lower federal court err in refusing to grant the government's request for mandatory, nondiscriminatory bulk-form sales of the drug and reasonable-royalty licensing of ICI and Glaxo patents as part of the relief to remedy the antitrust violations?

Decision: Yes to both questions. Opinion by Justice White. Vote: 6-3.

Reasons: Prior Supreme Court cases indicate that challenges to patent validity should be encouraged because "[i]t is as important to the public that competition should not be repressed by worthless patents, as that the patentee of a really valuable invention should be protected in his monopoly. . . ." Thus, the government should be permitted "to raise and litigate the validity of the ICI-Glaxo patents in this antitrust case," since the patents were directly involved in the antitrust violations. The Court noted, however, that the attorney general did not have "a roving commission to question the validity of any patent lurking in the background of an antitrust case." The Court also held that ICI and Glaxo should be required to sell the drug in bulk form "on reasonable and nondiscriminatory terms and to grant patent licenses at reasonable royalty rates to all bona fide applicants in order to 'pry open to competition' the griseofulvin market which 'has been closed by defendants' illegal restraints'." Otherwise, competition in the United States market for the drug would depend entirely on ICI's and Glaxo's "willingness to supply their present licensees with the bulk form of the drug."

Gulf States Utilities Company v. Federal Power Commission, 411 U.S. 747 (1973)

Facts: Over the objection of two Louisiana cities, the Federal Power Commission (Commission) refused to consider any anticompetitive effects in authorizing a public utility (Gulf States) to issue $30 million of 30-year bonds to refund part of its outstanding commercial paper and short-term notes. Section 204 of the Federal Power Act (Act) requires the Commission to find that issuance of a security by a utility is "compatible with the public interest" before approving it.

Question: When a public utility applies to the Commission for authority to issue securities, must the Commission, in passing upon the application under section 204 of the Act, consider the issue's anticompetitive effects?

Decision: Yes. Opinion by Justice Blackmun. Vote: 6-3.

Reasons: "Section 204 of the Act empowers the Commission to authorize the issuance of a security by a public utility *only* 'if it finds that such issue . . . is for some lawful object . . . and compatible with the public interest.'" Section 204 must be read together with companion statutes which were intended to curb the monopoly power of public utilities and to provide effective regulation of the expanding business of transmitting and selling electric power in interstate commerce. The Court thus concluded that the "public interest" standard of section 204 requires the Commission to consider both the financial and antitrust implications of a proposed security issue before authorizing its issuance.

Civil Rights. The Court decided eight cases in the growing area of federal civil rights litigation. In an important case arising under the federal Voting Rights

95

Act, the Court upheld the validity of the attorney general's regulations placing the burden on certain states to prove that any voting rule change, including state reapportionment plans, did not have a racially discriminatory purpose and would not have a discriminatory effect before the new rule could be implemented.

In a case having widespread significance for private clubs and individuals practicing racial discrimination in selling property or making contracts, the Court interpreted the 1866 and 1870 Civil Rights Acts to prevent the exclusion of Negroes from a community swimming club. The Court also suggested that the refusal to contract with a Negro on account of his race might also be deemed illegal.

The Court expanded the rights of private individuals to challenge discriminatory housing practices under the 1968 Civil Rights Act by holding that tenants of a segregated housing complex had standing to sue although not themselves the direct victims of discrimination.

Several cases involved the scope of 42 U.S. Code, 1983, which provides that "Every person who, under color of any statute, ordinance, regulation, custom, or usage, of any State or Territory," deprives any other person of a federal constitutional or statutory right shall be subject to a suit for damages, injunction or other appropriate relief. The Court ruled this term that section 1983 does not apply to action taken under District of Columbia law or by local government units.

Georgia v. United States, 411 U.S. 526 (1973)

Facts: Section 5 of the Voting Rights Act (Act), 42 U.S. Code, 1973b(b), applies to any state which employed on November 1, 1964, or on November 1, 1968, any of several enumerated tests as conditions to voting and in which less than 50 percent of the eligible voters were registered to vote or actually voted in the 1964 or 1968 presidential elections. It forbids these states from changing a "voting qualification or prerequisite to voting or standard practice or procedure with respect to voting" without first obtaining a declaratory judgment from the U.S. District Court for the District of Columbia that the proposed change "does not have the purpose and will not have the effect of denying or abridging the right to vote on account of race or color," *or* submitting the plan to the attorney general of the United States and receiving no objection within 60 days. Pursuant to statutory authority, the attorney general promulgated regulations which delayed the beginning of the 60-day period until the state submitted any documentation the attorney general requested, for the purpose of determining the effect of any proposed voting rule, and placed the burden on the state to prove that any such rule had no discriminatory purpose or effect. Georgia, a state covered by section 5 of the Act, submitted the 1972 legislative reapportionment plan for its House of Representatives to the attorney general for clearance on November 5, 1971. The attorney general requested more information regarding the proposed reapportionment plan, and it was received on January 6, 1972. Within 60 days, on March 3, 1972, the attorney general objected to the plan, concluding that its provisions for multimember districts, majority run-off elections, extensive departures from the state's prior policy of adhering to county lines, and other

96

changes created the possibility that it would have a racially discriminatory effect on voting. The State of Georgia nevertheless attempted to put its reapportionment plan into effect and the attorney general sued to enjoin its implementation. Georgia defended on grounds that: (1) section 5 of the Act did not apply to reapportionment plans, and (2) the attorney general's regulations regarding the tolling of the 60-day period and placing the burden of proof on the state to prove nonracially discriminatory purpose or effect were void.

Question: Did section 5 of the Act bar the State of Georgia from implementing its proposed 1972 legislative reapportionment plan?

Decision: Yes. Opinion by Justice Stewart. Vote: 6-3.

Reasons: In *Allen v. State Board of Elections,* 393 U.S. 544 (1969), the Court concluded that section 5 was "intended to reach any state enactment which altered the election law of a covered State even in a minor way." In a companion case, *Fairley v. Patterson,* the Court held that a change from district to at-large voting for county supervisor fell within the reach of section 5. When Congress amended the Voting Rights Act in 1970, it expressed no disapproval of *Allen* or *Fairley.* The Court thus concluded that in this case, in which the reapportionment plan had the potential for diluting the value of the Negro vote, the plan fell within the ambit of section 5.

The Court also upheld the validity of the two challenged regulations issued by the attorney general, finding that the regulations were a reasonable means of administering his obligations under section 5 of the Act.

Tillman v. Wheaton-Haven Recreation Association, Inc., 410 U.S. 431 (1973)

Facts: The Wheaton-Haven Recreation Association (Wheaton-Haven), a nonprofit corporation formed to operate a community swimming pool, limited the pool's use to white members and white guests. Although no one is guaranteed membership in Wheaton-Haven (approval by a majority of the board of directors is required for membership), under its bylaws a person residing within a three-quarter mile radius of the pool receives certain preferences for membership. Such a person needs no endorsement from a current member to be eligible for membership, receives priority (if the membership is full) in acquiring future membership and (if an owner-member is selling his house) can convey first option to purchase a membership to the buyer. A suit was brought against Wheaton-Haven by a Negro couple who bought a home in the three-quarter mile preference area but were denied membership for racial reasons, by white members whose Negro guest was refused admission to the pool for racial reasons, and by the Negro guest. They sued for damages and declaratory and injunctive relief against Wheaton-Haven on the ground that its racially discriminatory policies violated the 1866 and 1870 Civil Rights Acts (42 U.S. Code, 1982 and 1981, respectively) which give all citizens of the United States "the same right . . . to

. . . purchase, lease, sell, hold, and convey real and personal property" and "to make and enforce contracts."

Question: Did Wheaton-Haven's racially discriminatory membership and guest policies violate either the 1866 or 1870 Civil Rights Acts?

Decision: Yes. Opinion by Justice Blackmun. Vote: 9-0.

Reasons: In *Jones* v. *Alfred H. Mayer Co.,* 392 U.S. 409 (1968), the Court held that section 1982 forbade private acts of racial discrimination in connection with the transfer of real and personal property. In *Sullivan* v. *Little Hunting Park, Inc.,* 396 U.S. 229 (1969), the Court held that section 1982 forbade racial discrimination practiced by a corporation organized to operate a community park and playground facilities, including a swimming pool, for residents of a designated area. The facts of this case are indistinguishable from *Sullivan,* and thus Wheaton-Haven's racially discriminatory membership and guest policies must be deemed to violate section 1982. By determining that Wheaton-Haven was not intended to be a private establishment because it opened its membership to all white persons within a geographic area, the Court found it unnecessary to decide whether the broad language of section 1982 was narrowed by the 1964 Civil Rights Act whose anti-discrimination provisions are inapplicable to "private clubs."

The Court also in substance held that section 1981, giving all United States citizens the same right as white citizens "to make and enforce contracts," forbade private persons from refusing to contract with Negroes for racial reasons. The case was remanded to the district court to determine whether Wheaton-Haven's racially discriminatory guest policies as applied to the Negro guest and its white members violated their rights under section 1982 or 1981.

Trafficante v. Metropolitan Life Insurance Co., 409 U.S. 205 (1972)

Facts: Two tenants of an apartment complex, one black and one white, filed suit under section 810 of the 1968 Civil Rights Act alleging that their landlord discriminated against nonwhites, that the tenants thereby lost the social benefits of living in an integrated community and missed business and professional advantages that would have accrued from living with members of minority groups and suffered from being "stigmatized" as residents of a "white ghetto." The federal district court and court of appeals, without reaching the merits of the complaint, held that the complaining tenants were not entitled to sue under section 810 because they were not the alleged objects of discriminatory housing practices.

Question: Does section 810, which gives "[a]ny person who claims to have been injured by a discriminatory housing practice" a right to sue in federal court, mean that tenants have a right to sue even when they do not allege that they are the direct victims of discriminatory housing practices?

Decision: Yes. Opinion by Justice Douglas. Vote: 9-0.

Reasons: Although the 1968 Civil Rights Act gives the secretary of housing and urban development (HUD) power to receive and investigate complaints regarding discriminatory housing practices, court suits by private citizens are the primary method of obtaining compliance with the statute. This fact, the broad language of section 810, a review of the legislative history of that section, and HUD regulatory policies compel the conclusion that Congress intended, consistent with Article III of the Constitution giving federal courts jurisdiction only over "cases and controversies," that any tenant of a housing unit charged with discrimination be permitted to sue under section 810. Permitting all tenants of a housing complex to sue, even when they are not the direct victims of racial discrimination, does not pose any Article III problems because a deprivation of integrated housing quarters constitutes sufficient injury to tenants so that federal courts will not be deciding "abstract" questions of law in section 810 suits.

District of Columbia v. *Carter*, 409 U.S. 418 (1973)

Facts: Carter brought suit against District of Columbia police officers, alleging that they violated his civil rights under 42 U.S. Code, 1983, which provides that "[e]very person who, under color of any statute, ordinance, regulation, custom, or usage, of any State or Territory" violates a person's constitutional or federal rights shall be subject to a suit for damages or other appropriate judicial relief.

Question: Is the District of Columbia a "State or Territory" within the meaning of 42 U.S. Code, 1983 and thus may Carter's suit be properly maintained?

Decision: No. Opinion by Justice Brennan. Vote: 9-0.

Reasons: Section 1983 was passed primarily to enforce the provisions of the Fourteenth Amendment whose commands are addressed "only to the State or to those acting under color of its authority." In earlier cases, the Supreme Court had held the District of Columbia is not a "State" within the meaning of the Fourteenth Amendment. Thus, to conclude that section 1983 is inapplicable to the District of Columbia would be reasonable. After tracing the legislative hisory of section 1983, which was passed in the aftermath of the Civil War when the Ku Klux Klan had launched terrorist assaults against both blacks and known union sympathizers, the Court concluded that it was designed primarily "to afford a federal right in federal courts because, by reason of prejudice, passion, neglect, intolerance or otherwise, state laws might not be enforced and the claims of citizens to the enjoyment of rights, privileges, and immunities guaranteed by the Fourteenth Amendment might be denied by the state agencies."

Because Congress has always had plenary power to control and supervise District of Columbia officials by virtue of Article I, Section 8, clause 17 of the Constitution, the Court reasoned that the rationale of section 1983 was inapplicable to the District of Columbia, where the federal government could keep its own officers under control. Further, the District of Columbia could not be fairly compared with territories over which Congress had "confused and ineffective" control, thus "making the problem of enforcement of civil rights in the Territories more similar to the problem as it existed in the States than in the District of Columbia." The Court held that "in the absence of any indication in either the language, purposes or history of section 1983 of a legislative intent to include the district within the scope of its coverage, the conclusion is compelled" that the District of Columbia is not a "State or Territory" within the meaning of section 1983.

Kenosha v. Bruno, 412 U.S. 507 (1973)

Facts: After denial of their applications for renewal of their one-year liquor licenses by the cities of Racine and Kenosha, Wisconsin, retail liquor establishments sued those cities under 42 U.S. Code, 1983 alleging deprivation of their constitutional rights and seeking declaratory and injunctive relief. After the case reached the Supreme Court, the question arose as to whether a city could be sued under section 1983, which provides that "every person" who violates another's constitutional rights under color of state law may be sued for both legal and equitable relief.

Question: Is a city a "person" within the meaning of 42 U.S. Code, 1983 and thus subject to suit for either legal or equitable relief under that statute?

Decision: No. Opinion by Justice Rehnquist. Vote: 9-0.

Reasons: In *Monroe* v. *Pape,* 365 U.S. 167 (1961), the Court held that a city could not be sued for damages under section 1983 after examining the legislative history of that section. "We find nothing in the legislative history discussed in *Monroe,* or in the language actually used by Congress, to suggest that the word person in section 1983 was intended to have a bifurcated application to municipal corporations depending on the nature of the relief sought against them. Since, as the Court held in *Monroe,* 'Congress did not undertake to bring municipal corporations within the ambit of' . . . Section 1983 . . . they are outside of its ambit for purposes of equitable relief as well as for damages."

Moor v. Alameda County, 411 U.S. 693 (1973)

Facts: An Illinois citizen injured by Alameda County police in the process of quelling a civil disturbance sued Alameda County, California, under 42 U.S. Code, 1983 for damages in federal court contending that the county was vicariously liable for the acts of its police officers who allegedly violated the plaintiff's constitutional rights of free speech and assembly. Plaintiff contended that although *Monroe* v. *Pape,* 365 U.S. 167 (1961), held that a county could not be sued for damages under section 1983, Alameda County, vicariously liable for the acts of its police officials under California law, could be sued under 42 U.S. Code, 1988, which authorizes a federal court to adopt state remedies in federal civil rights suits if such remedies are not inconsistent with federal law. The Illinois citizen also contended he could sue Alameda County in federal court on his state law claims under 28 U.S. Code, 1332 giving federal courts jurisdiction to hear suits between citizens of different states.

Questions: If state law so permits, may a county be held liable for damages under 42 U.S. Code, 1988 despite the holding of *Monroe* v. *Pape* prohibiting damage suits against counties under 42 U.S. Code, 1983? Is Alameda County a "citizen" within the meaning of 28 U.S. Code, 1332 and thus liable to suit in federal court by an Illinois citizen?

Decision: No to the first question and yes to the second. Opinion by Justice Marshall. Vote: 8-1.

Reasons: The legislative history of section 1983 makes clear that Congress intended to hold counties immune from damage suits under that section. If section 1988 were interpreted to import state law *in toto* and to hold counties liable for damages, such result would be inconsistent with federal law as expressed in section 1983 and would thus be improper. The Court therefore held that Alameda County could not be sued for damages under section 1988, even though it might be sued for damages under state law.

The Court concluded that the Illinois plaintiff could assert his state law claims against Alameda County in federal court under 28 U.S. Code, 1332 because the county was a California citizen within the meaning of that federal diversity statute. Although a state is not a "citizen" for purposes of diversity jurisdiction, it is established law that political subdivisions, unless the arm or alter ego of the state, are citizens of their respective states for diversity purposes. After examining California law, the Court concluded that Alameda County had a sufficiently independent corporate character to justify treating it as a California citizen for federal diversity purposes.

McDonnell Douglas Corporation v. Green, 411 U.S. 793 (1973)

Facts: A Black civil rights activist was laid off by McDonnell Douglas Corporation (McDonnell) after having participated in protests against the corporation by illegally stalling cars on the main roads leading to its plant in order to block plant access. This former employee sued McDonnell under Title VII of the Civil Rights Act of 1964 claiming that his discharge was racially motivated and that McDonnell refused to rehire him as punishment for his protest of discriminatory working conditions at the plant. In deciding in favor of McDonnell, a lower federal court dismissed the employee's claim that his firing resulted from racial bias because the Equal Employment Opportunities Commission (EEOC) had earlier failed to find "reasonable cause" for this contention when the employee filed a complaint with EEOC.

Question: Does the absence of an EEOC finding of reasonable cause under Title VII of the 1964 Civil Rights Act bar suit in court under an appropriate section of that statute?

Decision: No. Opinion by Justice Powell. Vote: 9-0.

Reasons: The 1964 Civil Rights Act does not by its language restrict a complainant's right to sue to only those charges upon which the EEOC has made a finding of reasonable cause, and "we will not engraft on the statute a requirement which may inhibit the review of claims of employment discrimination in the federal courts."

In remanding the case to a lower federal court to determine whether the former black employee had been fired for racially discriminatory reasons, the Court stated that in a Title VII trial, a prima facie case of racial discrimination may be established by showing that the complainant (1) belongs to a racial minority, (2) applied and was qualified for a job for which the employer was seeking applicants, (3) was rejected, and (4) after rejection the position remained open and the employer continued to seek applicants from persons of complainant's qualifications. Once a prima facie case is established, the "burden then must shift to the employer to articulate some legitimate nondiscriminatory reason for . . . [the complainant's] rejection."

Northcross v. Memphis Board of Education, 412 U.S. 427 (1973)

Facts: Section 718 of the Emergency School Aid Act of 1972 provides that "[u]pon the entry of a final order by a court of the United States against a local educational agency, a State (or any agency thereof), or the United States (or any agency thereof)," in any action seeking to redress illegal or unconstitutional discrimination with respect to "elementary and secondary education, the court, in its discretion, upon a finding that the proceedings were necessary to bring about compliance, may allow the prevailing party, other than the United States, a reasonable attorney's fee as part of the costs." A lower federal court without opinion denied attorneys' fees under section 718 to plaintiffs who had successfully obtained desegregation of the Memphis public schools.

Question: Under section 718, should attorneys' fees ordinarily be awarded to successful plaintiffs unless special circumstances would render such an award unjust?

Decision: Yes. Per curiam opinion. Vote: 8-0.

Reasons: Section 718 tracks the wording of section 204(b) of the Civil Rights Act of 1964 which was interpreted to mean in *Newman* v. *Piggie Park Enterprises, Inc.,* 390 U.S. 400 (1968), that successful plaintiffs suing under that title "should ordinarily recover an attorney's fee unless special circumstances would render such an award unjust." The standard for determining whether attorneys' fees should be awarded under section 718 is the same standard used under section 204(b), not only because the language of the two statutes is similar, but because these statutes were both intended to encourage individuals injured by racial discrimination to seek judicial relief.

Consumer Credit. The Court struck a blow for consumer groups in upholding the validity of a Federal Reserve Board regulation requiring disclosure of certain credit terms whenever payment for goods was made in four or more installments.

Mourning v. Family Publication Service, Inc., 411 U.S. 356 (1973)

Facts: A purchaser bought magazine subscriptions from Family Publications Service (Service) under a contract calling for an immediate payment of $3.95 and a like sum to be paid monthly for 30 months. The contract failed to recite the total purchase price of the subscriptions and made no reference to service or finance charges. After defaulting on her monthly obligations, the purchaser sued Service under the Truth-in-Lending Act (Act) seeking recovery of a $100 statutory penalty on the ground that Service failed to comply with the disclosure provisions of section 121 of the Act, which required merchants regularly extending credit to disclose to all consumer credit customers, *inter alia,* the cash price of the merchandise sold, the amount of finance and other charges, and the rate of the charges. Pursuant to section 105 of the Act delegating to it broad power to promulgate regulations to facilitate compliance, the Federal Reserve Board (Board) promulgated Regulation Z requiring merchants to meet the disclosure requirements of the Act whenever credit is offered to a customer "for which either a finance charge is or may be imposed or which pursuant to an agreement, is or may be payable in more than four installments." Service defended on the ground that the "Four Installment Rule" of Regulation Z was invalid because unauthorized by section 105 of the Act.

Question: Did the Board exceed its authority under section 105 in promulgating the Four Installment Rule?

Decision: No. Opinion by Chief Justice Burger. Vote: 5-4.

Reasons: The legislative history of section 105 shows that Congress intended the Board to promulgate any regulations reasonably necessary to ensure that the disclosure objectives of the Act were not circumvented. The Board promulgated the Four Installment Rule to prevent creditors from avoiding the financial disclosure provisions of the Act through "burying" the cost of credit in the price of goods sold by charging higher cash prices. It is well established that regulations promulgated pursuant to a statute will be upheld if "reasonably related to the purposes of the enabling legislation." Because the Board's Four Installment Rule, although requiring disclosure in some sales transactions in which credit is in fact not extended, is reasonably related to the Act's objectives of encouraging disclosure of all financial charges whether or not such charges are buried in the price of goods, the Court concluded that the rule must be upheld. The fact that the rule forces disclosure in some transactions where credit is not extended did not render it invalid.

Environmental Law. In an environmental case arising under the Rivers and Harbors Act of 1899, the Court upheld the power of the government absolutely to forbid the discharge of refuse into navigable waters. In another environmental case, the Court divided 4-4 on the important question of whether the Clean Air Act authorizes the Environmental Protection Agency to prevent a state from allowing any significant deterioration in the air quality of relatively clean areas even though the resulting air quality level would be cleaner than that required for already polluted areas. In this case, *Frei* v. *Sierra Club*, the tie vote produces no opinion.

In two other cases involving state and local authority over the environment, the Court upheld the power of states to regulate oil spills but struck down a local ordinance regulating "noise pollution" from jet aircraft.

United States v. Pennsylvania Industrial Chemical Corporation, 411 U.S. 655 (1973)

Facts: Charged with violating section 13 of the Rivers and Harbors Act of 1899 (Act) prohibiting the discharge into navigable waters of certain refuse matter, the Pennsylvania Industrial Chemical Corporation (PICCO) raised the defenses that: (1) the secretary of the army had failed to establish a formal regulatory-permit program as permitted by section 13 for authorizing the discharge of refuse into navigable waters, and (2) the Army Corps of Engineers had consistently construed section 13 as limited to those deposits that would impede or obstruct navigation, thereby affirmatively misleading PICCO into believing that a section 13 permit was not required as a condition to the discharges involved in this case. A lower federal court found PICCO guilty of violating section 13 and rejected PICCO's defenses.

Question: May a defendant in a criminal prosecution under section 13 of the Act raise as a defense: (1) the failure of the secretary of the army to establish a permit program to authorize the discharge of refuse into navigable waters in certain circumstances, or (2) the fact that the consistent construction put on section 13 by the Army Corps of Engineers affirmatively misled the defendant into thinking his conduct was not criminal?

Decision: No to the first defense and yes to the second. Opinion by Justice Brennan. Vote: 7-2.

Reasons: "[W]hile nothing in Section 13 precludes the establishment of a formal regulatory [permit] program by the Secretary [of the Army], it is equally clear that nothing in the section *requires* the establishment of such a program as a condition to rendering Section 13 operative." Nothing in the language of section 13, its legislative history, or its relation to other federal water pollution laws justifies the conclusion that the absence of a formal regulatory-permit program permissible under section 13 precludes prosecution for violation of its provisions.

The Court, however, accepted PICCO's contention that it could defend the criminal prosecution under section 13 on the ground that the long-standing Army Corps of Engineers' interpretation of section 13 limited its prohibition to water deposits that tend to impede or obstruct navigation and thereby affirmatively misled PICCO into believing that its conduct was not criminal. Noting that the Supreme Court had earlier held in *United States* v. *Standard Oil Co.*, 384 U.S. 224 (1966), that section 13 of the 1899 act could be validly applied to any discharge into navigable waters causing pollution and not just to discharges obstructing or impeding navigation, the Court nevertheless concluded that if the Army Corps of Engineers, through its regulations, had consistently construed section 13 as limited to discharges impeding navigation, it would have deprived PICCO of fair warning as to what conduct the government intended to make criminal under that section. If PICCO lacked fair warning, traditional notions of fairness inherent in our system of criminal justice would therefore prevent the government from proceeding with the prosecution. The case was thus remanded to the lower court to determine whether this latter defense could be established.

Askew v. American Waterways Operators, Inc., 411 U.S. 325 (1973)

Facts: Florida's Oil Spill Prevention and Pollution Control Act (Florida Act) imposed strict liability for any damage incurred by the state or private persons as a result of an oil spill in the state's territorial waters from any waterfront facility used for drilling oil or handling the transfer or storage of oil and from any ship destined for or leaving such facility. This Florida Act was challenged as unconstitutional on the ground that it regulated conduct preempted by the Water Quality Improvement Act (Federal Act), the Admiralty Extension Act, and the federal maritime power under the Constitution. The Florida Act also provided for state regulation of containment gear and other equipment maintained by ships and terminal facilities for the prevention of oil spills. The Federal Act authorized the President to promulgate regulations requiring ships and terminal facilities to maintain equipment for the prevention of oil spills and subjected shipowners and terminal facilities to liability without fault up to $14 million and $8 million, respectively, for cleanup costs incurred by the federal government (but not other entities) as a result of oil spills. The Admiralty Extension Act provided for federal maritime jurisdiction over "all cases of damage or injury . . . caused by a vessel on navigable water" even though such damage or injury was consummated on land.

Question: Is the Florida Act unconstitutional under the Supremacy Clause of Article VI because preempted by either the Federal Act, the Admiralty Extension Act, or federal constitutional power over maritime activities?

Decision: No. Opinion by Justice Douglas. Vote: 9-0.

Reasons: The Federal Act specifically provides that it shall not be construed to preempt a state from imposing "any requirement of liability" respecting the discharge of oil into its waters. Thus, the Florida Act, which imposes greater liability for oil spills upon terminal facility licensees and shipowners than does the Federal Act, is not inconsistent with the Federal Act. Moreover, without any concrete dispute regarding the same, the Florida Act's provisions requiring "containment gear" on ships cannot be deemed invalid per se under the Commerce Clause on the ground that the subject to be regulated requires uniform federal regulation.

The Admiralty Extension Act, which extends federal jurisdiction over all sea-to-shore injuries, was not intended to preempt state regulation of sea-to-shore

105

pollution, "historically within the reach of the police power of the State. . . ." Thus, the Florida Act is in no way barred by the Admiralty Extension Act.

The contention that the federal constitutional maritime power impliedly preempted the Florida Act was rejected by the Court which reasoned that prior case law clearly established that states may modify or supplement maritime law if not "hostile to the characteristic features of maritime law or inconsistent with federal legislation." Because the Florida Act did not interfere with maritime matters requiring uniform federal regulation and was not otherwise inconsistent with federal legislation, the Court upheld its constitutionality.

Burbank v. Lockheed Air Terminal, Inc., 411 U.S. 624 (1973)

Facts: An ordinance adopted by the city council of Burbank made it unlawful for a so-called pure jet aircraft to take off from the Hollywood-Burbank Airport between 11 p.m. of one day and 7 a.m. of the next day and made it unlawful for the operator of that airport to allow them to take off during such periods. The ordinance was challenged as unconstitutional under the Supremacy Clause because it was inconsistent with the Federal Aviation Act and the Noise Control Act providing for comprehensive federal regulation of airspace, aircraft, and air safety.

Question: Is the challenged city ordinance, intended to regulate a local aircraft noise problem, unconstitutional under the Supremacy Clause because it was inconsistent with comprehensive federal regulation of airspace and air safety as expressed in the Federal Aviation Act and the Noise Control Act?

Decision: Yes. Opinion by Justice Douglas. Vote: 5-4.

Reasons: Section 1348 of the Federal Aviation Act gives the administrator of the Federal Aviation Administration (FAA) broad authority to regulate the use of navigable airspace "in order to insure the safety of aircraft and the efficient utilization of such airspace . . ." and "for the protection of persons and property on the ground. . . ." The district court found that the imposition of curfew ordinances on a nationwide basis would cause a bunching of flights in the hours preceding the curfew thereby increasing air congestion and air noise during that time. The challenged curfew ordinance would interfere with the federal aviation administrator's power to promote the efficient utilization of airspace and to regulate the aircraft noise problem in consultation with the Environmental Protection Agency under the 1972 Noise Control Act. Although nothing in either the Federal Aviation Act or the Noise Control Act expressly preempts local curfew ordinances, "the pervasive nature of the scheme of federal regulation of aircraft noise" compels the conclusion that preemption of such curfew ordinances was intended. The Court thus concluded that the challenged local curfew ordinance was preempted by federal regulation and noted that "[i]f we were to uphold the Burbank ordinance and a significant number of municipalities followed suit, it is obvious that fractionalized control of the timing of take-offs and landings would severely limit the flexibility of the FAA in controlling air traffic flow."

Federal Tort Claims. In a unanimous 9-0 decision, the Court refused to expand the liability of the United States under the Federal Tort Claims Act by holding that it was not liable for the negligence of independent contractors performing services for the government.

Logue v. United States, 412 U.S. 521 (1973)

Facts: A federal prisoner committed suicide while confined in a county jail pending trial. His parents sued the United States under the Federal Tort Claims Act (FTCA) claiming that negligence on the part of government agents and employees proximately caused the death of their son. The FTCA generally makes the federal government liable for the negligence of its agents and employees but excludes government liability for the negligence of employees of independent contractors performing services for the government. Because the suicide was allegedly caused by the negligence of county jail employees, who were supervising the federal prisoner under a contract between the Federal Bureau of Prisons and the county, the government claimed that the suit fell outside the FTCA because none of its employees or agents was responsible for the suicide.

Question: Were the allegedly negligent county jail officials either government agents or employees for purposes of the FTCA?

Decision: No. Opinion by Justice Rehnquist. Vote: 9-0.

Reasons: Under the FTCA, the federal government is liable for the negligence of its employees whose physical conduct it has authority to control, but is not liable for the negligence of the employees of independent contractors over whom the government has no supervisory authority in the performance of the contract. In this case, the county jail in return for a fee provided for the safekeeping, care and subsistence of federal prisoners. Because the county operated the day-to-day operations of its jail without federal supervision or control, it clearly was an independent contractor under the FTCA, and thus the federal government was not liable for the negligence of the county jail employees.

The Court also rejected the argument that the county jail employees were acting on behalf of the federal government because they performed duties the government would otherwise be required to perform and thus were government agents under the FTCA. If this were the law, the Court noted, the exclusion of government liability for the negligence of employees of independent contractors would be "virtually meaningless, since it would be a rare situation indeed in which an independent contractor with the Government would be performing tasks that would not otherwise be performed by salaried Government employees."

Food and Drug Law. In a series of cases, the Court upheld the broad power of the Food and Drug Administration to ban the sale of drugs unless proven by scientific evidence to be both effective and safe.

Weinberger v. Hynson, Westcott, and Dunning, Inc., 412 U.S. 609 (1973)

Facts: The 1962 amendments to the Food, Drug and Cosmetic Act (Act) defined a "new drug" as a drug not generally recognized among experts as effective or safe for its intended uses, thereby expanding the prior definition of new drug which included only drugs not generally recognized as safe. Under the Act, a new drug may not be marketed unless a new drug application (NDA) has been approved. The Food and Drug Administration (FDA) is directed to refuse approval of an NDA and to withdraw any prior approval if substantial evidence is lacking that the drug is effective for its intended use. Under the amendments, all NDAs approved prior to 1962 were deemed approved for a two-year period during which manufacturers could gather substantial evidence of their effectiveness. The 1962 amendments also contained a "grandfather clause" exempting certain drugs from the effectiveness requirement. To aid in reviewing the effectiveness of all marketed drugs, the FDA used data gathered by the National Academy of Sciences—National Research Council. After providing an opportunity for a hearing, the FDA ordered the drug Lutrexin off the market for failure to show any substantial evidence that it was effective. The producer of the drug (Hynson) sought a declaratory judgment in federal district court that Lutrexin was exempt from the effectiveness requirements, or alternatively that it submitted enough evidence of efficacy to warrant a full hearing before the FDA removed Lutrexin from the market. A lower federal court rejected Hynson's first contention but accepted the second.

Questions: Was Lutrexin exempt from the efficacy requirements of the Act? Was there sufficient evidence of Lutrexin's effectiveness to warrant a full hearing before the FDA prior to removal from the market?

Decision: No to the first question and yes to the second. Opinion by Justice Douglas. Vote: 7-0.

Reasons: Although the FDA need not hold a hearing before removing a drug for lack of effectiveness when the applicant has not tendered any acceptable evidence on the matter, in this case Hynson submitted enough evidence to justify a full hearing on the effectiveness of Lutrexin.

The Court rejected the contention, however, that Lutrexin was exempt from the effectiveness requirements of the Act. Although Lutrexin had been approved for marketing in 1953, the 1962 amendments to the Act required it to meet the effectiveness standards therein within two years. The Court concluded that the "grandfather clause" exemption covered only drugs that had never been subject to new drug regulation and thus did not exempt Lutrexin which had been subject to FDA regulation before the 1962 amendments to the Act. The Court added that "a drug can be 'generally recognized' by experts as effective for intended use within the meaning of the Act only when that expert consensus is founded upon" substantial evidence derived from studies meeting the scientific standards established by the FDA.

USV Pharmaceutical Corp. v. Weinberger, 412 U.S. 655 (1973)

Facts: A drug manufacturer sought a declaratory judgment that certain drugs it produced were exempt from the "effectiveness" requirements under section 107(c)(4) of the 1962 amendments to the Food, Drug and Cosmetics Act (Act) essentially because the disputed drugs were either generally recognized as safe before the 1962 amendments or had never been covered by a new drug application (NDA) approved by the Food and Drug Administration (FDA). A lower federal court rejected the manufacturer's contention, concluding that even if the disputed drugs were generally recognized as safe before 1962 they were still subject to the 1962 amendments.

Question: Were the disputed drugs, generally recognized as safe before the 1962 amendments to the Act, nevertheless subject to the "effectiveness" requirements of the amendments?

Decision: Yes. Opinion by Justice Douglas. Vote: 7-0.

Reasons: The 1962 amendments (1) redefined a "new drug" as one not generally recognized by experts as both safe and effective or one that had not been used to a material extent for a material time, (2) required affirmative FDA approval for NDAs whereas previously NDAs automatically became effective unless a contrary order was issued, (3) required FDA disapproval of an NDA if there is a lack of substantial evidence that the drug will have the effect it purports or is represented to have, and (4) required that any previous approval of an application be withdrawn whenever it appears from new information or otherwise that there is a lack of substantial evidence of the drug's effectiveness. Under this scheme, drugs previously approved by the FDA before 1962 could stay on the market until the NDA was withdrawn, and a minimum of two years was provided for submission of substantial evidence proving the drug's effectiveness before any such withdrawal. The Court thus concluded that the disputed drugs were subject to the "effectiveness" requirements of the Act.

The Court also noted that all "me-too" copies of an NDA drug—all drugs of a similar composition—are subject to the efficacy requirements to the same extent as the NDA product itself.

Weinberger v. Bentex Pharmaceuticals, 412 U.S. 645 (1973)

Facts: Several drug manufacturers sought a declaratory judgment that a certain drug (pentylenetetrazol) was exempt from the "effectiveness" requirements of the 1962 amendments to the Food, Drug and Cosmetic Act (Act) on the grounds that the drug's safety and effectiveness had been determined prior to the amendments and that it fell within the "grandfather clause" exemption. The Food and Drug Administration (FDA) had ordered the drug removed from the market, as well as all drugs of similar composition known as "me-too" drugs, on the ground that no substantial evidence of their effectiveness had been shown. A federal appeals court held that whether the drugs were "new drugs" within the meaning of the Act and thus subject to its effectiveness requirements should be determined by the district court, which had referred the issue to the FDA.

Question: Did the federal district court have authority to refer to the FDA the question of whether the disputed drugs were "new drugs" within the meaning of the Act?

Decision: Yes. Opinion by Justice Douglas. Vote: 7-0.

Reasons: Although in some circumstances orders of the FDA are reviewed by federal courts of appeal, the Court stated that review by a federal district court was also permissible under the Administrative Procedure Act. In this case, the district court properly deferred the difficult "new drug" questions to the FDA which has special expertise in the matter. The Court rejected the contention that the FDA had no jurisdiction, either primary or concurrent, to decide in an administrative proceeding what is a "new drug" which must meet both the safety and effectiveness requirements of the Act.

Labor Law. The Court in decisions this term both expanded and contracted the power of labor unions to punish union members. In striking a blow at labor union power, the Court held that unions had no power to punish former members for acts committed after they had resigned from the union. On the other hand, the Court held that the National Labor Relations Board had no power to inquire into the reasonableness of union disciplinary fines assessed against current union members.

In a suit having widespread importance, which concerned the immunity of states from damage suits under the Eleventh Amendment, the Court held that individual state employees were not authorized to sue state agencies for violation of the Fair Labor Standards Act.

NLRB v. Granite State Joint Board, Textile Workers, 409 U.S. 213 (1972)

Facts: After a union struck its employer and voted to fine any member $2,000 who aided or abetted the employer during the strike, 31 of its members who had participated in the vote resigned from the union and returned to work while the strike continued. (Neither the union's constitution nor bylaws contained any provision defining or limiting the circumstances under which a member could resign.) After the union imposed fines on all 31 employees who had resigned from the union and returned to work, the National Labor Relations Board charged the union with an unfair labor practice in violation of section 8 (b)(1) of the National Labor Relations Act (NLRA) which prohibits unions from coercing employees who refuse to engage in concerted activities.

Question: Did the union commit an unfair labor practice under section 8(b)(1) of the NLRA when it imposed fines on the 31 employees who had resigned from the union before they violated the union resolution against aiding the employer during the strike?

Decision: Yes. Opinion by Justice Douglas. Vote: 8-1.

Reasons: In *NLRB* v. *Allis-Chalmers Mfg. Co.,* 388 U.S. 175 (1967), the Court held that a union did not violate section 8(b)(1) by fining members enjoying full union membership who worked during a lawful strike authorized by the membership. However, "when a member lawfully resigns from the union its power over him ends." Section 8(b)(1) protects an employee against union interference with his "right to refrain from any or all" concerted activities relating to collective bargaining or mutual aid and protection. Thus, "[w]here a member lawfully resigns from a union and thereafter engages in conduct which the union proscribes, the union commits an unfair labor practice when it seeks enforcement of fines for that conduct."

Booster Lodge No. 405 v. NLRB, 412 U.S. 84 (1973)

Facts: The National Labor Relations Board (NLRB) held that a union committed an unfair labor practice under section 8(b)(1)(A) of the National Labor Relations Act (NLRA) by seeking court enforcement of fines imposed upon ex-members for strikebreaking activities occurring after their resignation from the union, even though the union constitution expressly prohibited members from strikebreaking.

Question: Was the NLRB's decision proper?

Decision: Yes. Per curiam opinion. Vote: 9-0.

Reasons: In *NLRB* v. *Granite State Joint Board, Textile Workers,* 409 U.S. 213 (1973), the Court held that "[w]here a member lawfully resigns from a union and thereafter engages in conduct which the union proscribes, the union commits an unfair labor practice when it seeks enforcement of fines for that conduct." Since in that case there was no provision in the union's constitution or bylaws limiting the circumstances in which a member could resign, the Court concluded that the members were free to resign at will and that section 7 of the NLRA protected their right to return to work during a strike which had been commenced while they were union members. The union's imposition of court-collectible fines against the former members for such work was therefore held to violate section 8(b)(1)(A).

In this case, as in *Granite State,* the union's constitution and bylaws were silent on the subject of voluntary resignation from the union, and the Court thus concluded that union members were free to resign at any time. Finding that the union's constitutional prohibition against strikebreaking by members did not extend to nonmembers who had recently resigned, the Court reasoned that the case was governed by *Granite State* and thus held that the union's seeking court enforcement of fines for acts by former union members after they resigned constituted an unfair labor practice.

NLRB v. Boeing Co., 412 U.S. 67 (1973)

Facts: A lower federal court held that an unreasonably large fine assessed by a union against some of its members for strikebreaking activities which violated the union constitution was an unfair labor practice under section 8(b)(1) (A) of the National Labor Relations Act (NLRA) because such large fines coerced and restrained employees from exercising their right under section 7 of the NLRA to refrain from striking. The National Labor Relations Board (NLRB) had ruled that an inquiry into the reasonableness of a disciplinary fine assessed by a union upon some of its members for purposes of determining whether a union had committed an unfair labor practice was forbidden under section 8(b) (1)(A) of the NLRA which gives a union the right to "prescribe its own rules with respect to the acquisition or retention of membership therein."

Question: Does section 8(b)(1)(A) of the NLRA prohibit an inquiry by the NLRB into the reasonableness of a union disciplinary fine when the NLRB exercises its authority under that section to determine whether the fine otherwise constitutes an unfair labor practice?

Decision: Yes. Opinion by Justice Rehnquist. Vote: 6-3.

Reasons: In *Scofield* v. *NLRB*, 394 U.S. 423 (1969) and *NLRB* v. *Allis-Chalmers Mfg. Co.,* 388 U.S. 175 (1967), the Court held that section 8(b)(1) (A) was not intended to give the NLRB power to regulate internal union affairs, including the imposition of disciplinary fines and their consequent court enforcement against members who violate the union's constitution and bylaws. An inquiry by the NLRB into the reasonableness of a union fine would "necessarily lead the Board to a substantial involvement in strictly internal affairs" by examining the union's motivation for imposing the fine. The Court thus held that the size of a union fine per se can never be an unfair labor practice under section 8(b)(1)(A) of the NLRA. The Court noted that state courts would be free to apply state law to issues concerning the reasonableness of union fines in suits brought by either the union or the member fined.

NLRB v. International Van Lines, 409 U.S. 48 (1972)

Facts: For refusing to cross a picket line formed in connection with a union's organizing campaign, four employees of International Van Lines were fired. After determining that the labor picketing was activity protected under section 7 of the National Labor Relations Act (NLRA) and that the discharges were unfair labor practices in violation of sections 8(a)(1) and 8(a)(3) of the NLRA (which prohibit employers from discriminating against employees who engage in union activity or other concerted action), the National Labor Relations Board (NLRB) ordered the four discharged employees reinstated with back pay. When the four employees were discharged International Van Lines did not hire any permanent replacements.

Question: Was the NLRB's remedial order of reinstatement with back pay proper?

Decision: Yes. Opinion by Justice Stewart. Vote: 9-0.

Reasons: "It is settled that an employer may refuse to reinstate economic strikers if in the interim he has taken on permanent replacements. It is equally settled that employees striking in protest of an employer's unfair labor practices are entitled, absent some contractual or statutory provision to the contrary, to unconditional reinstatement with back pay even if replacements for them have been made." In this case the Court concluded that the discharged employees were entitled to reinstatement with back pay because the "discharges themselves" were unfair labor practices.

Brennan v. Arnheim & Neely, Inc., 410 U.S. 512 (1973)

Facts: The secretary of labor sued a real estate management company (Arnheim) for alleged violations of the Fair Labor Standards Act (FLSA) which provides for certain minimum wages, overtime compensation, and recordkeeping. Managing eight commercial office buildings and one apartment complex in the Pittsburgh area on behalf of their owners, Arnheim negotiated leases with tenants, instituted legal actions respecting the leases, collected rent, and conducted the hiring, firing, payroll operations, and job supervision of the maintenance and janitorial staffs. Arnheim defended on the ground that under section 3(s) of the FLSA, the statute did not apply to an enterprise, as defined in section 3(r), with less than $250,000 gross sales after January 31, 1969. Arnheim contended that its management activities at all of the nine buildings served should not be aggregated as part of a single "enterprise" under section 3(r) for purposes of determining whether its gross sales brought it within the coverage of the FLSA under section 3(s).

Question: Should all Arnheim's management activities at the buildings it served be aggregated as part of a single "enterprise" within the meaning of section 3(r) of the FLSA?

Decision: Yes. Opinion by Justice Stewart. Vote: 8-1.

Reasons: Section 3(r) defines enterprise as "the related activities performed (either through unified operation or common control) by any person . . . for a common purpose, and includes all such activities whether performed in one or more establishments. . . ." The three main elements of the statutory definition of "enterprise" are related activities, unified operation or common control, and common business purpose. Arnheim is the employer of all of the building employees it supervises; its activities in all of the buildings are virtually identical and are plainly related; and its activities are under common control being directed from a central office. Thus, all Arnheim's management activities were part of a single "enterprise" under section 3(r).

Employees v. Department of Public Health and Welfare of Missouri, 411 U.S. 279 (1973)

Facts: State employees of the Missouri Department of Public Health and Welfare sued the State of Missouri under section 16(b) of the federal Fair Labor Standards Act (FLSA) seeking overtime compensation and liquidated damages in a like amount. (Under the FLSA, certain state hospitals and mental health institutions are required to pay certain overtime compensation to state employees for hours worked in excess of 40 per week.) The lower federal court dismissed the complaint on the ground that it was barred by the Eleventh Amendment which deprives federal courts of jurisdiction to hear suits brought by private citizens against states.

Question: Does section 16(b) of the FLSA permit state employees of hospitals and mental health institutions to sue a state in federal court without its consent notwithstanding the Eleventh Amendment?

Decision: No. Opinion by Justice Douglas. Vote: 6-3.

Reasons: Under the Eleventh Amendment, "an unconsenting State is immune from suits brought in federal courts by its own citizens as well as by citizens of another State." Although Congress intended to bring employees of state hospitals within the coverage of the minimum wage and overtime provisions of the FLSA, the legislative history of that statute indicates Congress did not intend that private citizens be permitted to enforce those provisions under section 16(b) of the FLSA and thereby attempt to remove state immunity under the Eleventh Amendment. Under section 17, the secretary of labor may enjoin violations of the FLSA and obtain restitution in behalf of state employees "for suits by the United States against a State are not barred by the Constitution." Since a holding that state employees could sue states under section 16(b) would subject states to potentially enormous new fiscal burdens, only the most explicit statement by Congress that this effect was intended could lead the Court to conclude that section 16(b) attempted to override state immunity under the Eleventh Amendment. The Court thus did not reach the question of whether Congress could, consistent with the Eleventh Amendment, subject a state to suit by state hospital employees under section 16(b) of the FLSA.

In *Parden* v. *Terminal R. Co.,* 377 U.S. 184 (1964), the Court held that the Federal Employees' Liability Act (FELA), which permitted employees of state-owned railroads to sue states for damages in federal courts, did not violate the Eleventh Amendment because by choosing to operate railroads states waived their immunity from suit under that amendment. Although the Court rested its decision in *Employees* v. *Department of Public Health and Welfare of Missouri* on statutory construction of section 16(b) of the FLSA, it nevertheless chose to distinguish *Parden* on the grounds that the FELA regulated "proprietary" railroads and not nonprofit hospitals, and that the FELA remedy compensated state railroad employees only to the extent of their actual damages whereas the FLSA provided for double damages. The Court thus left open the possibility that new legislation by Congress unambiguously permitting state employees of hospitals to sue states under section 16(b) of the FLSA would be unconstitutional under the Eleventh Amendment.

Patents. In a patent case significant for the computer industry, the Court held that certain computer software programs were unpatentable but did not rule out granting patents to other types of computer programs.

Gottschalk v. Benson, 409 U.S. 63 (1972)

Facts: Two employees of Bell Laboratories sought a patent for a computer program related "to the processing of data by program and more particularly to the programmed conversion of numerical information" in general purpose digital computers. The employees argued that their method for converting binary-coded-decimal (BCD) numerals into pure binary numerals qualified as a "process" that was patentable under 35 U.S. Code, 101 which provides: "Whoever invents or discovers any new and useful process . . . may obtain a patent."

Question: Does the computer programming method developed by the Bell Laboratory employees qualify as a "process" within the meaning of the Patent Act, 35 U.S. Code, 100(b) which provides: "The term 'process' means process, art or method, and includes a new use of a known process, machine, manufacture, composition of matter, or material?"

Decision: No. Opinion by Justice Douglas. Vote: 6-0.

Reasons: The patent sought is on a method of programming a general purpose digital computer to solve certain types of mathematical problems according to a mathematical formula (algorithm). However, "an idea itself is not patentable." Concluding that if a patent were granted for the computer method of converting BCD numerals to pure binary numbers, "the patent would wholly preempt the mathematical formula and in practical effect would be a patent on the algorithm itself," the Court held that the conversion "process" was too close to an idea to be patentable. The Court made clear, however, that its decision did not rule out the granting of patents to other types of computer programs.

Securities Regulation. In the securities field, the Court rejected the contention that the insider-trading rules in section 16(b) of the Securities Exchange Act should be mechanically enforced but instead adopted a case-by-case approach requiring a determination of whether any possible abuse of inside information was possible in each case.

Kern County Land Co. v. Occidental Petroleum Corp., 411 U.S. 582 (1973)

Facts: Section 16(b) of the Securities Exchange Act (Act) provides that holders of more than 10 percent of the listed stock of any company shall be liable to that company for any profits realized from any purchase and sale (or sale and then purchase) of the company's stock occurring within a six-month period. Pursuant to a tender offer, Occidental Petroleum Corporation (Occidental) became a holder of more than 10 percent of the stock of Kern County Land Company (Old Kern) on May 10, 1967. To frustrate Occidental's takeover attempt, Old Kern merged with Tenneco on August 30, 1967, under terms providing that shareholders of Old Kern would receive a share of Tenneco cumulative preference stock in exchange for each share of Old Kern common stock which they owned. To avoid being locked into a minority position in Tenneco, Occidental had earlier negotiated an agreement between May 30 and June 2,

1967, with Tenneco whereby Occidental granted Tenneco an option to purchase at $105 per share all of the Tenneco preference stock to which Occidental would be entitled pursuant to the merger terms ultimately agreed upon on August 30, 1967. Tenneco paid some $8 million to secure the option which would be applied to the purchase price if the option was exercised, but Tenneco was not entitled to exercise the option until six months and one day after Occidental became a more than 10 percent owner of Old Kern common stock. After Tenneco exercised its option and Occidental realized a profit of about $20 million on the sale of Old Kern stock, New Kern (the Tenneco subsidiary corporation owning all of Old Kern's assets) sued to recover the $20 million under section 16(b) on the theories that (1) Occidental's exchange of Old Kern stock for Tenneco stock pursuant to the merger on August 30, 1967, was a "sale" within the meaning of that section and was made within six months of Occidental's purchase of more than 10 percent of Old Kern's stock on May 10, 1967, and (2) the option agreement between Occidental and Tenneco executed on June 2, 1967, constituted a "sale" of Old Kern stock by Occidental.

Question: Did either the exchange of Old Kern stock pursuant to the merger agreement or the granting to Tenneco of an option to purchase the stock received in the exchange by Occidental constitute a "sale" within the meaning of section 16(b), thereby subjecting Occidental to liability for profits realized in these transactions?

Decision: No. Opinion by Justice White. Vote: 6-3.

Reasons: The purpose of section 16(b) is to prevent the unfair use of inside information about companies by persons having an especially close relation to that company—officers, directors, and holders of more than 10 percent of its stock. The word "sale'" in section 16(b) must be interpreted in a manner consistent with the section's purpose. In this case, Occidental had practically no involvement either in Old Kern's decision to merge with Tenneco or in the terms of that merger. Although rejecting the notion that an exchange of stock pursuant to a merger could never result in section 16(b) liability, the Court stated that "the involuntary nature of Occidental's exchange [of Old Kern stock for Tenneco stock], when coupled with the absence of the possibility of speculative abuse of inside information" in the exchange compelled the conclusion that section 16(b) was not intended to apply to the challenged transaction in this case.

The Court also rejected the contention that the option agreement constituted a "sale" within the meaning of section 16(b), reasoning that the $8 million premium did not make the exercise of the option economically inevitable and thus tantamount to a sale. Moreover, since the option only entitled Tenneco to purchase its own stock and since Occidental was not an "insider" of that company, the Court concluded that there existed no possibility for Occidental to use inside information in a manner that section 16(b) was intended to prevent.

Taxation. Two federal tax cases this term were particularly notable. In one, the

Court concluded that mutual fund shares should be valued at their redemption price rather than sales price for estate tax purposes. In the other, the Court concluded that an elaborate scheme established by a group of physicians working in partnership to provide retirement benefits for the group could not avoid a current tax on the payments going into the retirement trust fund.

United States v. Cartwright, 411 U.S. 546 (1973)

Facts: The Internal Revenue Code of 1954 (Code) requires that for estate tax purposes the "value" of all property held by a decedent at the time of death be included in the gross estate. A treasury regulation valuing all shares in open-end mutual funds at their public offering price (which generally includes an 8 percent sales charge) instead of at their redemption price (which is lower by the amount of the sales charge) was challenged as being unrealistic and unreasonable and therefore void. Shares in an open-ended mutual fund can only be redeemed from the issuing company at a price excluding the sales charge.

Question: Is the contested treasury regulation valuing open-ended mutual fund shares at their public offering price for estate tax purposes unreasonable and thus invalid?

Decision: Yes. Opinion by Justice White. Vote: 6-3.

Reasons: For estate tax purposes, the value of property is determined by the price at which the property would change hands between knowledgeable, willing buyers and sellers. However, under the Investment Company Act, mutual fund shares may be "sold" back to the fund only at the redemption price. Thus, free market economic principles do not operate at the time of redeeming the mutual fund shares. Nevertheless, the most reasonable economic analysis of the redemption transaction is that it represents what a willing buyer and willing seller agreed upon at the time of the purchase of the mutual fund. Thus, mutual fund shares should be valued at their redemption price for estate tax purposes. The contested treasury regulation, which imputes to the value of mutual fund shares a sales charge which can never be recovered by the shareholder is unreasonable and does not comport with economic reality. Although declaring the contested treasury regulation invalid, the Court reaffirmed the principle that treasury regulations must be upheld if found to implement a congressional mandate found in the Code in "some reasonable manner."

United States v. Basye, 410 U.S. 441 (1973)

Facts: A group of physicians formed a medical partnership (Permanente) and contracted to supply medical services to members of a health foundation (Kaiser). Pursuant to the agreement, a portion of the compensation paid to Permanente by Kaiser was in the form of unconditional, unrecoverable payments into a retirement trust for the benefit of Permanente's physicians. Under the terms of the retirement trust, however, no physician was eligible to receive his portion of the trust fund unless he: (1) was retired, had rendered at least 15 years of continuous service and had attained age 65, (2) rendered his professional services only to Kaiser, and (3) honored any reasonable Kaiser request to render consultative services to any Kaiser operated health plan. Permanente did not report Kaiser's trust fund payments as income in its partnership returns nor did its individual members include these payments in computations of their distributive shares of the partnership's taxable income. The commissioner of internal revenue assessed income tax deficiencies against each Permanente partner on the theory that Kaiser's payments to the trust were current compensation to the partnership for the services it rendered and that the partners were taxable on their distributive share of that compensation, notwithstanding the deflection of that compensation to the retirement trust and its current unavailability to the partners.

Question: Were the Kaiser trust fund payments income to Permanente and thus properly taxable as income to the partners according to their distributive shares of those payments?

Decision: Yes. Opinion by Justice Powell. Vote: 8-1.

Reasons: Section 703 of the Internal Revenue Code of 1954 (Code) provides in relevant part that "[t]he taxable income of a partnership shall be computed in the same manner as in the case of an individual." Once a partnership's income is ascertained and reported, its existence may be disregarded for income tax purposes because each partner pays taxes on his portion of the total partnership income as if the partnership were merely a conduit through which the income passed. (A partnership as an entity pays no income taxes.) The unrecoverable trust payments made by Kaiser to Permanente were undisputably payments for medical services rendered and thus income to Permanente under section 61 (a) (1) of the Code, which provides that gross income includes "compensation for services. . . ." Although Kaiser's trust payments were available only to fund Permanente's retirement plan and were not otherwise usable by it, Permanente was nevertheless properly taxable for such payments under the principle established in *Lucas* v. *Earl,* 281 U.S. 111 (1930), that he who earns income is taxable on it even though he deflects such income to other persons. "Since the retirement fund payments should have been reported as income to [Permanente] . . . the individual partners should have included their shares of that income in their individual returns . . . [f]or it is axiomatic that each partner must pay taxes on his distributive share of the partnership's income without regard to whether that amount is actually distributed to him."

The Court rejected the contention that "each partner's distributive share prior to retirement was too contingent and unascertainable to constitute presently recognizable income." Noting that the Congress had provided different tax treatment of pension plans for corporate employees than it provided for the self-employed and members of partnerships, the Court concluded that the partners must pay income tax on their respective shares of the payments made to the retirement trust.

United States v. Chicago, Burlington & Quincy Railroad Co., 412 U.S. 401 (1973)

Facts: Prior to 1954, a railroad company (CB&Q) received, at public expense, highway undercrossings and overcrossings, crossing signals, signs, floodlights, jetties and bridges. These capital assets were carried on the railroad's books at the cost incurred by the federal and state governments to build them. CB&Q successfully contended before the Court of Claims that these capital assets built at public expense were nonshareholder contributions to capital under section 113(a)(8) of the Internal Revenue Code of 1939, and thus it was entitled to claim a depreciation deduction for these assets under section 23(1). (As a general rule, taxpayers may take a depreciation deduction for capital assets used in their trade or business. In this case, the depreciation deduction was proper if the assets were contributions to capital under section 113(a)(8)).

Question: Were these CB&Q assets (acquired at public expense) nonshareholder contributions to capital within the meaning of section 113(a)(8) of the Internal Revenue Code of 1939?

Decision: No. Opinion by Justice Blackmun. Vote: 6-2.

Reasons: The cases of *Detroit Edison Co.* v. *Commissioner,* 319 U.S. 98 (1943) and *Brown Shoe Co.* v. *Commissioner,* 339 U.S. 583 (1950) provide the standard for determining the characteristics of a nonshareholder contribution to capital under the Internal Revenue Code. "It certainly must become a permanent part of the transferee's working capital structure. It may not be compensation, such as a direct payment for a specific, quantifiable service provided for the transferor by the transferee. It must be bargained for. The asset transferred foreseeably must result in benefit to the transferee in an amount commensurate with its value. And the asset ordinarily, if not always, will be employed in or contribute to the production of additional income and its value assured in that respect." In this case, CB&Q did not bargain for the publicly subsidized capital assets. Any incremental economic benefit to CB&Q from the assets was marginal. And the assets were peripheral to CB&Q's main business and did not materially contribute to the production of income. The assets were constructed "primarily for the benefit of the public to improve safety and to expedite traffic flow." The Court thus concluded that the governmentally subsidized capital assets did not constitute nonshareholder contributions to CB&Q's capital under section 113(a)(8) of the 1939 Code.

Fausner v. Commissioner, 413 U.S. 838 (1973)

Facts: A commercial airline pilot who regularly traveled by private automobile from his home to his place of employment unsuccessfully sought to deduct the entire cost of commuting for income tax purposes under section 162 (a) of the Internal Revenue Code (Code) on the theory that such expenses were incurred to transport his flight bag and overnight bag and thus constituted ordinary and necessary business expenses.

Question: Are commuting expenses deductible under section 162(a) of the Code merely because the taxpayer must carry incidentals of his occupation with him?

Decision: No. Per curiam opinion. Vote: 9-0.

Reasons: Section 262 of the Code prohibits the deduction of "personal" expenses which have long been held to include commuting expenses. Perhaps if the transport of job-required tools and material to and from work leads to additional commuting expenses, then the allocation of commuting costs between "personal" and "business" expenses may be feasible. But no such allocation can be made in this case.

United States v. Chandler, 410 U.S. 257 (1973)

Facts: When the decedent purchased several Series E United States Savings Bonds in 1954, she had them issued in co-ownership form with her granddaughters. In 1961, the decedent delivered these bonds to the granddaughters with the intent of making an irrevocable inter vivos gift but without complying with valid treasury regulations permitting legal transfer of the jointly issued bonds so long as both co-owners were alive but only through reissuance at the request of both co-owners. When the decedent died in 1962, the government included in her gross estate for estate tax purposes the Series E bonds she delivered to her granddaughters in co-ownership form. Section 2040 of the Internal Revenue Code provides that a decedent's gross estate shall include "the value of all property . . . to the extent of the interest therein held as joint tenants by the decedent and any other person . . . in their joint names and payable to either or the survivor. . . ." (Since the deceased paid for the bonds, under section 2040 the value of all and not just one-half of the bonds was included in her gross estate.) The deceased's estate sued for a refund of the estate tax attributable to the inclusion of the bonds in her gross estate.

Question: Does a registered co-owner of a Series E savings bond by physical delivery of the bond to the other registered co-owner, with intent to effectuate an inter vivos gift but without reissuance of the bond, succeed in divesting himself of the incidents of ownership so that at his subsequent death the value of the bond is not includable in his gross estate under the joint interests provisions of section 2040 of the Internal Revenue Code of 1954?

Decision: No. Per curiam opinion. Vote: 9-0.

Reasons: The decedent "chose not to have the bonds in question reissued in the names of her granddaughters as she might have done pursuant to the applicable regulations." The treasury regulations restricting transfer were not unreasonable in view of the "requirements of government for uniformity and for proper record keeping" in dealing with over $50 billion of outstanding Series E bonds, 75 percent of them registered in co-ownership form. The decedent was not unfairly taxed on the bonds because until her death she "retained the right to redeem each of the bonds in question, the right to succeed to the proceeds if she survived the putative donee, and the right to join or to veto any attempt to have the bond reissued."

Welfare. The most significant decision in the field of welfare concerned the constitutionality of New York's work rules designed to encourage welfare recipients to get jobs. The Court upheld the validity of the work rules over the claim that they were constitutionally preempted by a comparable federal work incentive program. The Court reasoned that the federal and state programs had the same goals and concluded that Congress did not intend to stifle states in seeking ways to decrease the burdens of welfare.

New York State Department of Social Services v. Dublino, 413 U.S. 405 (1973)

Facts: As a condition to receiving federal aid under federal welfare statutes, states that administer welfare programs must provide that certain employable individuals register for manpower services, training and employment under regulations promulgated by the secretary of labor (the WIN program). In addition to the WIN program, the state of New York established work rules requiring employable welfare recipients to report every two weeks to pick up their assistance checks in person, to comply with an employment referral system, and to work in public works projects. Failure of those recipients to comply with the work rules resulted in a loss of federally supported welfare benefits. The New York work rules were challenged as unconstitutional because allegedly preempted by the federal WIN program.

Question: Are the New York work rules preempted by the federal WIN program?

Decision: No. Opinion by Justice Powell. Vote: 7-2.

Reasons: The purpose of both the work rules and WIN is to help individuals on welfare acquire a sense of dignity by becoming wage earners. The determination of whether the work rules are preempted by WIN must be made in light of a federal welfare program giving states maximum latitude in allocating welfare funds and emphasizing a scheme of cooperative federalism. Neither the language of the statute creating WIN nor its legislative history gives any indication that it was intended to preempt state work programs. Moreover, WIN is capable of serving only a fraction of New York's social service districts. "It would be incongruous for Congress on the one hand to promote work opportunities for [welfare] recipients and on the other hand to prevent States from undertaking supplemental efforts toward this very same end." Finding no friction between New York's work rules and the federal WIN program, the Court concluded that the former was not preempted by the latter.

Philpott v. Essex County Welfare Board, 409 U.S. 413 (1973)

Facts: As a condition to receiving welfare assistance under New Jersey law, a recipient must execute an agreement to reimburse the county welfare board for all payments received. (The statute's apparent purpose was to enable welfare boards to obtain reimbursement out of subsequently discovered or acquired real and personal property of the recipient.) After a recipient executed the required agreement in order to receive disability benefits under New Jersey law, he was awarded retroactive disability insurance benefits under the Social Security Act, benefits which he deposited in his bank account. When the welfare board sued to recover the social security money in his bank account under the agreement to reimburse, the recipient defended on the ground that the suit was barred by virtue of 42 U.S. Code, 407, which provides that social security "moneys" shall not be subject to "execution, levy, attachment, garnishment, or other legal process."

Question: Does 42 U.S. Code, 407 bar the welfare board's suit to recover the recipient's social security "moneys" under the recipient's agreement to reimburse the board for all assistance received?

Decision: Yes. Opinion by Justice Douglas. Vote: 9-0.

Reasons: "On its face the Social Security Act in Section 407 bars the State of New Jersey from reaching the federal disability payments paid to [the recipient]. . . . [T]he funds on deposit [with the bank] were readily withdrawable and retained the quality of 'moneys' within the purview of Section 407." The Court concluded that section 407 banned all creditor claims from reaching social security moneys and that an exemption for state creditors could not reasonably be inferred.

Miscellaneous Constitutional Cases

In important cases that defy overall constitutional categorization, the Court handed down decisions concerning congressional immunity and congressional reapportionment, copyrights, state powers of taxation, and the definition of "just compensation."

In a case involving the scope of the Speech or Debate Clause, the Court held that congressmen and their aides were within its protection when sued for alleged libelous acts in having a subcommittee report published and distributed. However, under the Court's decision certain Government Printing Office officials might be subject to suit for publicly distributing the report.

The Court reaffirmed its strict one-man, one-vote rule as applied to congressional reapportionment plans in striking down a Texas scheme having only a 3 percent variation in population equality among districts.

The question of what factors could be considered in setting "just compensation" for property taken by eminent domain arose in two cases. By 5-4 votes in both cases, the Court left the constitutional issues nearly as unresolved as it found them.

Congressional Reapportionment

White v. *Weiser*, 412 U.S. 783 (1973)

Facts: A Texas congressional reapportionment plan providing for a maximum population variation among districts of approximately 3 percent was successfully challenged as unconstitutional in violation of the one-man, one-vote principle mandated by Article I, Section 2 of the Constitution.

Question: Did the Texas congressional reapportionment plan violate the one-man, one-vote principles of Article I, Section 2 of the Constitution because of its 3 percent variation in population equality among districts?

Decision: Yes. Opinion by Justice White. Vote: 9-0.

Reasons: Article I, Section 2 of the Constitution provides that representatives be chosen "by the People of the several States." Prior case law has interpreted that section to permit population variances among congressional districts only if "unavoidable." Because Texas failed to prove that the 3 percent population deviations among congressional districts was "unavoidable," its proposed reapportionment plan is unconstitutional.

The Court also ruled, however, that the lower court should have selected the reapportionment plan that more closely adhered to the state legislature's plan from two alternatives before it, both of which met constitutional standards.

Congressional Immunity

Doe v. *McMillan*, 412 U.S. 306 (1973)

Facts: Pursuant to a resolution of the House of Representatives, the Select Subcommittee of the Committee on the District of Columbia investigated the District of Columbia public school system and issued a 450-page report to the Committee of the Whole House. Thereafter, the House ordered the report to be printed and distributed to the public by the Government Printing Office. Claiming the report contained libelous statements about them, various parents and children sued the following persons, among others, seeking damages and an injunction against further distribution of the report: (1) the chairman and members of the House Committee on the District of Columbia, (2) the clerk, staff director, and counsel of the committee, (3) a consultant and an investigator for the committee, and (4) the superintendent of documents and the public printer. These defendants claimed they were immune from the suit under the Speech or Debate Clause of the United States Constitution, Article I, Section 6, clause 1 or under official immunity doctrine.

Question: Were the congressmen, their aides, and the Government Printing Office defendants absolutely immune from the libel suit under the Speech or Debate Clause or official immunity doctrine?

Decision: All defendants, except those from the Government Printing Office, are absolutely immune from this suit. Opinion by Justice White. Vote: 5-4.

Reasons: The purpose of the Speech or Debate Clause is to "prevent intimidation of legislators by the executive and accountability before a possibly hostile judiciary . . ." and the clause absolutely protects a member of Congress from suit for any conduct within the "sphere of legitimate legislative activity." Prior case law makes clear that voting by members, issuing committee reports, and member conduct at legislative committee hearings may not be made the basis for a civil or criminal judgment against a member. Moreover, *Gravel* v. *United States,* 408 U.S. 606 (1972), makes clear that the Speech or Debate Clause protects a member's aides insofar as the aides' conduct would be a protected legislative act if performed by the member. "[T]he complaint in this case was barred by the Speech or Debate Clause insofar as it sought relief from the Congressmen-Committee members, from the committee staff, from the consultant, or from the investigator, for introducing material at committee hearings that identified particular individuals, for referring the report that included the material to the Speaker of the House, and for voting for publication of the report. Doubtless, also, a published report may, without losing Speech or Debate Clause protection, be distributed to and used for legislative purposes by Members of Congress, congressional committees, and institutional or individual legislative functionaries. At least in these respects, the actions upon which petitioners sought to predicate liability were 'legislative acts,' and, as such, were immune from suit."

The Court then turned to the question of whether the acts of the Government Printing Office (GPO) defendants in printing and publicly distributing the challenged report at the request of the House of Representatives were also protected by the Speech or Debate Clause. Reasoning that the GPO defendants were members' aides under the *Gravel* doctrine, the Court nevertheless concluded that the Speech or Debate Clause affords no absolute immunity from private suit to persons who, with authorization from Congress, distribute materials which allegedly infringe upon the rights of individuals. Rejecting the contention that because public dissemination of the report was integral to the legislative function of informing the public and it therefore fell within the Speech or Debate Clause immunity, the Court stated that the test of immunity was whether the acts are "an integral part of the deliberative and communicative processes by which Members participate in committee and House proceedings" regarding legislative or other matters before the House. The Court stated that public dissemination of the report might be unprotected if it was unnecessary to congressional performance of its proper legislative functions. The Court remanded the case to the lower federal court to determine whether the challenged acts of the GPO defendants were within the Speech or Debate Clause protection under the standards it set forth in this case.

The Court also rejected the claim that the GPO defendants were absolutely immune from suit under *Barr* v. *Matteo,* 300 U.S. 564 (1959), which conferred such immunity upon certain governmental officials for discretionary acts committed within the outer perimeter of their authority. Whether absolute immunity should be conferred depends on whether its contribution "to effective government in particular contexts outweighs the perhaps recurring harm to individual citizens. . . ." Although the acts of printing and publicly disseminating the report fell within the statutory authority of the GPO defendants, the Court concluded that their challenged acts were basically nondiscretionary, and would have been unprotected if performed by a department head who ran the printing press and distributed the documents, and thus should be deemed outside the immunity doctrine of *Barr* v. *Matteo*.

Copyrights

Goldstein v. *California*, 412 U.S. 546 (1973)

Facts: Convicted of committing acts of "record piracy" or "tape piracy" in 1970-71 under a California statute proscribing such acts, the defendants unsuccessfully challenged the constitutionality of that statute on grounds that it conflicted with Article I, Section 8, clause 8 of the Constitution, the "Copyright Clause," and the federal statutes enacted thereunder. (Federal law did not grant copyright protection for sound recordings until February 15, 1972. Record or tape piracy is generally accomplished by purchasing certain popular tapes or phonograph records at retail, duplicating the tapes or records on blank tapes, and then winding the duplication on a cartridge for resale to retail outlets.) The challenged California statute prohibited the transference of any performance fixed on a tape or record onto other records or tapes with the intention of selling the duplicates, unless having first received permission from those who, under state law, are the owners of the master recording.

Question: Is the California "tape piracy" statute unconstitutional as applied to acts committed in 1970-71 because in conflict with either the Copyright Clause of the Constitution or federal statutes enacted pursuant thereto which did not, until February 15, 1972, provide copyright protection for sound recordings?

Decision: No. Opinion by Chief Justice Burger. Vote: 5-4.

Reasons: Article I, Section 8, clause 8 of the Constitution gives Congress the power "[t]o promote the Progress of Science and useful Arts by securing for limited Times to Authors and Inventors the exclusive Right to their respective Writings and Discoveries. . . ." The principle underlying the formation of the Constitution, that the federal government is one of limited powers, establishes that states are constitutionally prohibited from exercising authority only where the Constitution (1) expressly grants the union an exclusive authority, (2) explicitly denies the state an authority, or (3) grants the union an authority to which a similar authority in the state would be absolutely and totally contradictory and repugnant. The first two instances mentioned do not preclude state copyright statutes because the Copyright Clause neither expressly grants exclusive power to issue copyrights to Congress nor prohibits the states from exercising such power. The Court also concluded that state copyright statutes were not necessarily repugnant to national copyright power because the Copyright Clause addressed itself only to artistic creations of national importance but not to creations of local importance. State copyright statutes may further the purposes of the Copyright Clause by encouraging persons to devote themselves to intellectual and artistic creation without impinging upon the power of other states to permit unlimited access to such creations. The Court thus held that the challenged California tape piracy statute, creating copyright protection for sound recordings, was not forbidden by the Copyright Clause of the Constitution.

Turning to the question of whether federal copyright statutes, at least before 1972, were intended to preempt the challenged California statute, the Court concluded that the failure of Congress to forbid or provide copyright protection for sound recordings while doing so for other artistic creations showed that Congress intended to permit states to regulate copyright protection for sound recordings. "[U]nless Congress takes further action with respect to recordings fixed prior to February 15, 1972, the California statute may be enforced against acts of piracy" occurring before that date.

Just Compensation

Almota Farmers Elevator & Warehouse Co. v. *United States*, 409 U.S. 470 (1973)

Facts: The Almota Farmers Elevator and Warehouse Co. (Company) leased land adjacent to a railroad to conduct grain elevator operations. It had extensive buildings and other improvements on the leased land. With seven and one-half years to run on the current lease, the government condemned the Company's leasehold interest. For determining "just compensation" as required by the Fifth Amendment, the Company contended that the likelihood that the lease would have been renewed should be considered in valuing the buildings and improvements on the land whose useful life was considerably longer than the seven and one-half years remaining in the lease term.

Question: Upon condemnation of a leasehold, is a lessee with no right of renewal entitled to receive as compensation the market value of its improvements without regard to the limitation of the remaining term of the lease because of the expectancy that the lease would have been renewed?

Decision: Yes. Opinion by Justice Stewart. Vote: 5-4.

Reasons: "The Fifth Amendment provides that private property shall not be taken for public use without 'just compensation.' " The owner of condemned property is constitutionally entitled to its monetary equivalent which is normally "ascertained from what 'a willing buyer would pay in cash [for the property] to a willing seller.' " Because the Company had had its lease renewed continually since 1919, a private buyer would probably have bought the leasehold at a price reflecting the use of the improvements on the land over their useful life on the assumption the leasehold would continue to be renewed. Thus, since a private buyer would have paid the Company for its improvements valued in part on the possibility that the lease would be renewed, so must the government under the constitutional mandate to pay "just compensation" for property condemned.

United States v. Fuller, 409 U.S. 488 (1973)

Facts: In a condemnation proceeding brought by the United States to take 920 acres of a rancher's lands, adjacent to federal land on which he was entitled to graze livestock by virtue of a revocable permit issued under the Taylor Grazing Act (Grazing Act), the rancher successfully contended that the "just compensation" requirement of the Fifth Amendment entitled the jury fixing compensation to consider the value accruing to the land because of its actual or potential use in combination with the Grazing Act's "permit" lands. The Grazing Act authorizes the secretary of the interior to issue revocable permits to livestock owners for grazing their stock on federal government lands (permit lands), but provides that its provisions "shall not create any right, title, interest, or estate in or to the lands."

Question: Does the Fifth Amendment's provision for "just compensation" require the government to pay the rancher for that element of value in the condemned land which is based upon the use of the land in combination with the government's Grazing Act permit lands?

Decision: No. Opinion by Justice Rehnquist. Vote: 5-4.

Reasons: "The constitutional requirement of just compensation derives as much from the basic equitable principles of fairness . . . as it does from technical concepts of property law." Noting, however, that such a principle could not be pushed to its logical conclusion, as when a jury considers as an element of value a parcel's proximity to a post office building, the Court stated that generally "the Government as condemnor may not be required to compensate a condemnee for elements of value which the Government had created, or which it might have destroyed under the exercise of governmental authority other than the power of eminent domain." Since the government could revoke Grazing Act permits without paying compensation, the Court concluded the government was not constitutionally required to compensate the rancher for the added value of his land because of its proximity to permit lands.

State Taxing Powers

Evco v. Jones, 409 U.S. 91 (1972)

Facts: Evco, a private New Mexico corporation, employed writers, artists and draftsmen to develop educational instructional programs generally consisting of reproducible originals of books, films and magnetic audio tapes. Contracts were negotiated for the sale of Evco's educational programs and such programs were delivered outside New Mexico. When New Mexico levied its emergency school tax and gross receipts tax on the total proceeds Evco received from its educational program sales, Evco disputed the assessments in New Mexico state courts arguing that such taxes levied on out-of-state sales of tangible personal property imposed an unconstitutional burden on interstate commerce in violation of Article I, Section 8, clause 3 of the Constitution.

127

Question: Do New Mexico's taxes levied against the gross receipts of Evco's out-of-state sales of tangible personal property impose an unconstitutional burden on interstate commerce in violation of Article I, Section 8, clause 3, which gives Congress plenary power to "regulate Commerce . . . among the several States . . ."?

Decision: Yes. Per curiam opinion. Vote: 9-0.

Reasons: "Our cases indicate that a State may tax the proceeds from services performed in the taxing State, even though they are sold to purchasers in another State. But a tax levied on the gross receipts from sales of tangible personal property is an impermissible burden on commerce." In *J. D. Adams Mfg. Co.* v. *Storen,* 304 U.S. 307 (1938), the Court held that a State gross receipts tax on a taxpayer's sale of road machinery to out-of-state customers was unconstitutional and stated that the vice of the statute was that, if lawful, it would expose interstate commerce to a double tax burden to which intrastate commerce was not exposed.

Since the New Mexico state courts had established that Evco's educational programs were tangible personal property, the Court reasoned that *J. D. Adams Mfg. Co.* compelled the conclusion that New Mexico's gross receipts taxes levied on Evco's out-of-state sales of its educational programs violated the Commerce Clause of the Constitution.

Heublein, Inc. v. South Carolina Tax Commission, 409 U.S. 275 (1972)

Facts: The South Carolina Tax Commission assessed Heublein, Inc., a Connecticut corporation producing alcoholic beverages, a total of $21,549.50 in taxes on income derived from the sale of goods in South Carolina. Heublein challenged the legality of the state taxes on the ground that they violated 15 U.S. Code, 381 which prohibits states from imposing a net income tax on taxpayers whose income derived within the state is the result of shipping tangible personal property in interstate commerce pursuant to orders solicited within the state. As required by state law, Heublein had a local distributor in South Carolina receive its shipments from Connecticut and distribute its Connecticut goods to liquor wholesalers.

Question: Does the South Carolina net income tax as applied to Heublein violate the provisions of 15 U.S. Code, 381?

Decision: No. Opinion by Justice Marshall. Vote: 8-0.

Reasons: Section 381 provides that no state shall levy a net income tax on income derived within the state from interstate commerce if the recipient of the income confines its business within the state to "the solicitation of orders . . . in such State, for sales of tangible personal property, which orders are sent outside the State for approval or rejection, and, if approved, are filled by shipment or delivery from a point outside the State." Heublein, however, has not merely solicited orders for its Connecticut liquor in South Carolina but has "sent its products to a local representative who transferred them to a local wholesaler" within South Carolina. This transfer within South Carolina was neither "solicitation" nor the filling of orders "by shipment or delivery from a point outside the State" under section 381. Although Heublein "transferred" its liquor to a wholesaler in South Carolina instead of selling it directly at retail solely because a South Carolina statute so required, the Court reasoned that the transfer requirement within the state was not designed to evade the "mere solicitation" limits of section 381 but to permit the state to regulate the sale of liquor more easily. Thus, the Court concluded that section 381 did not "prohibit the taxation of Heublein's local sales" because South Carolina had an independent valid regulatory purpose in requiring Heublein to undertake more than mere solicitation as a condition of selling liquor within the state.

United Air Lines, Inc. v. Mahin, 410 U.S. 623 (1973)

Facts: United Air Lines, Inc. (United) challenged the constitutionality of an Illinois personal property use tax as applied to aviation fuel purchased in Indiana and stored in Illinois for two to twelve days before it was loaded aboard aircraft and consumed on interstate flights. United contended that the Illinois use tax levied on all the aviation fuel stored for use in interstate flights, not just upon that portion consumed in Illinois, unconstitutionally burdened interstate commerce.

Question: Does the Illinois personal property use tax levied upon all aviation fuel stored there for use in interstate flights unconstitutionally burden interstate commerce?

Decision: No. Opinion by Justice Blackmun. Vote: 6-3.

Reasons: In *Edelman* v. *Boeing Air Transport, Inc.,* 289 U.S. 249 (1933), the Court upheld a state gasoline use tax imposed on gasoline imported from outside the state, stored in tanks at an airport, and loaded aboard planes departing on interstate flights. In *Nashville, Chattanooga & St. Louis R. Co.* v. *Wallace,* 288 U.S. 249 (1933), the Court upheld a Tennessee privilege tax levied on oil purchased outside Tennessee by a railroad for use as a motive fuel in the railroad's interstate and intrastate operations. In this case, the taxable "use" of the aviation fuel under the challenged Illinois statute is either storage or withdrawal from storage. *Edelman* and *Nashville* compel the conclusion that the Illinois use tax "as applied to all fuel withdrawn from storage for consumption in an interstate vehicle, does not place an unconstitutional burden on interstate commerce." The Court noted that the likelihood of double taxation of the fuel was minimal because it could not be taxed by states through which it is transported under *Michigan-Wisconsin Pipe Line Co.* v. *Calvert,* 347 U.S. 157 (1964), nor by the state in which it is consumed under *Helson* v. *Kentucky,* 279 U.S. 245 (1929). Such a distribution of taxing power achieves a fair result "because a State in which preloading storage facilities are maintained is likely to provide substantial services to those facilities, including police protection and the maintenance of public access roads."

McClanahan v. Arizona State Tax Commission, 411 U.S. 164 (1973)

Facts: Arizona imposed its personal income tax on a reservation Indian whose entire income was derived from reservation sources and rejected the contention that the tax interfered with matters which the relevant treaty and statutes left exclusively to the province of the federal government and the Indians themselves.

Question: Is the Arizona personal income tax unlawful as applied to reservation Indians with income derived wholly from reservation sources?

Decision: Yes. Opinion by Justice Marshall. Vote: 9-0.

Reasons: "The policy of leaving Indians free from state jurisdiction and control is deeply rooted in the Nation's history." Indian reservations have long been deemed separate but dependent nations within the union with the power of regulating their internal and social relations. The relevant 1868 treaty between the United States government and the Navajo nation precluded any extension of state tax law to Indians on the Navajo reservation. Subsequent federal statutes indicate Congress' intent to maintain the tax exempt status of reservation Indians.

Mescalero Apache Tribe v. Jones, 411 U.S. 145 (1973)

Facts: New Mexico levied a gross receipts tax on a ski resort operated by the Mescalero Apache Tribe (Tribe) outside the boundaries of the Tribe's reservation on land leased from the United States Forest Service and a use tax on certain personal property purchased out of state and used in connection with the resort.

Question: Does the Constitution or paramount federal law permit the state's levy of a gross receipts tax on the ski resort operations located outside the Tribe's boundaries or of a use tax on personal property used in connection with the resort?

Decision: Only the gross receipts tax is permissible. Opinion by Justice White. Vote: 6-3.

Reasons: "[E]ven on [Indian] reservations state laws may be applied unless such application would interfere with reservation self-government or would impair a right granted or reserved by federal law. . . . Even so, in the special area of state taxation, absent cession of jurisdiction or other federal statutes permitting it" a state may not tax Indian reservation lands or Indian income derived from activities conducted within reservation boundaries. But, absent express federal law to the contrary, Indians going beyond reservation boundaries are properly "subject to nondiscriminatory state law otherwise applicable to all citizens of the State." No federal statute precluded the state's levy of a gross receipts on the Tribe's off-reservation ski resort and thus such tax is not invalid under the Supremacy Clause.

The Court also rejected the contention that the Indian Reorganization Act of 1934 (Act), which encouraged tribes to revitalize self-government and to achieve economic self-sufficiency through creation of chartered corporations with powers to conduct tribal business, rendered the Tribe's ski resort a federal instrumentality constitutionally immune from state taxes under *McCulloch* v. *Maryland,* 17 U.S. 316 (1819). Reasoning that the Act was intended to disentangle tribes from official bureaucracy and encourage Indian initiative, the Court concluded that Congress did not intend off-reservation tribal enterprises to be deemed "an arm of the government" and thus federal instrumentalities immune from state taxation.

Regarding the state's use tax, the Court held that 25 U.S. Code, 465 specifically forbade such tax on the Tribe's personal property that had been installed in the construction of ski lifts and thereby became permanently attached to the Tribe's realty. Section 465 exempts from state and local taxation "any lands" taken in the name of the United States in trust for an Indian tribe. The personal property taxed by the state was "land" within the meaning of section 465 because it had become a permanent improvement thereon. Although the land on which the tribal ski resort was located was not held in trust for them by the United States, the Tribe's lease of the land from the United States Forest Service was sufficient to bring the land within the immunity of section 465.

United States v. State Tax Commission of Mississippi, 412 U.S. 363 (1973)

Facts: A Mississippi regulation required out-of-state liquor distillers and suppliers to collect and remit to the state a wholesale markup on liquor sold to officers' clubs, ship stores, and post exchanges located on two military bases over which the United States exercised exclusive jurisdiction. Under Mississippi law, the state was the exclusive wholesaler of alcoholic beverages distributed within the state, and it collected a markup of 17-20 percent on all sales to retailers. It was the 17-20 percent wholesale markup charged to the retailers that out-of-state liquor dealers selling directly to the post exchanges upon the two military bases were required to collect. The United States unsuccessfully challenged the regulation in lower federal court contending that it constituted an attempt by the state to legislate with respect to military facilities and territory over which the Congress has exclusive legislative authority and therefore violated Article I, Section 8, clause 17 of the Constitution.

Question: Does Article I, Section 8, clause 17 of the Constitution prohibit the challenged regulation which in effect imposes a nondiscriminatory tax upon out-of-state distillers and suppliers of liquor selling directly to post exchanges on military bases within the exclusive jurisdiction of the United States?

Decision: Yes. Opinion by Justice Marshall. Vote: 7-2.

Reasons: Article I, Section 8, clause 17 empowers Congress to "exercise exclusive Legislation . . . over all Places purchased by the Consent of the Legislature of the State in which the Same shall be, for the Erection of Forts, Magazines, Arsenals, dock-Yards, and other needful Buildings." The tracts of land upon which the military bases are located were purchased pursuant to the provisions of Article I, Section 8, clause 17. Prior case law makes clear that, even considering the Twenty-first Amendment (giving states broad authority to regulate the sale of liquor within their jurisdiction), the challenged regulation is invalid because it attempts to regulate transactions involving the wholesale sale of liquor which occur wholly outside the state's jurisdiction. The transactions, strictly between the United States and out-of-state distillers and suppliers, involve goods ordered by officers' clubs and delivered within the military bases over which the United States claims exclusive jurisdiction.

The Court noted, however, that Mississippi maintained authority under the Twenty-first Amendment to regulate both liquor shipments through the state to the extent necessary to prevent its unlawful diversion into local commerce and the transportation of liquor off the two military bases. The Court remanded the case to the lower court to consider other issues raised by its ruling.

INDEX OF CASES